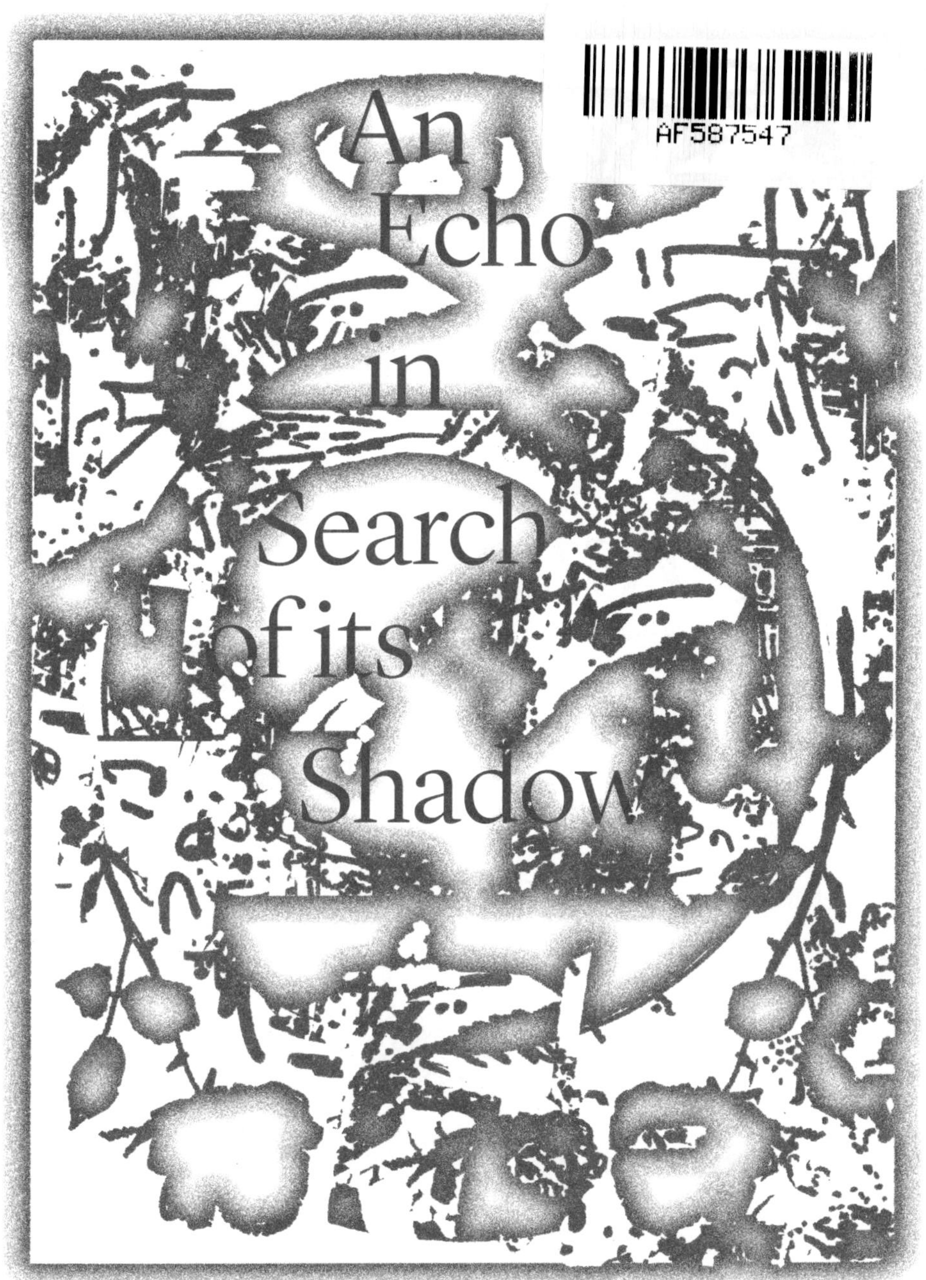

Aesthetics of the Repressed

Adam HajYahia &
Haitham Haddad

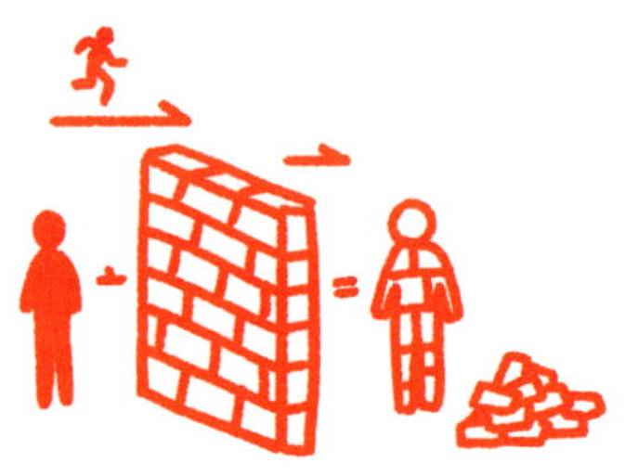

Preface

Aesthetics

of the

جمالك جمال مش عادي

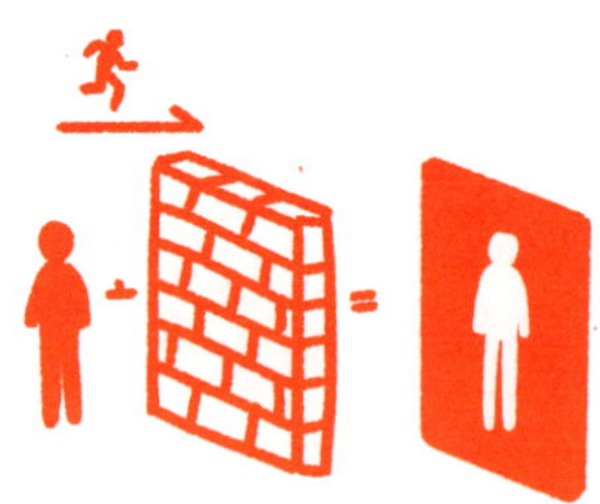

Repressed

او جماليّات المكبوت

There is something that happens in uprisings and revolutions that isn't merely implicit. How and why are people simultaneously awakened—especially in a contemporary society defined by alienation, consumption, and individualism—without any prior planning? How do we rise at the same time and in the same manner if, prior to the culminating long-awaited event, we had been leading separated liberalized lives? After all, despite our fragmented struggling, not all of us are embedded in struggle, neither are we all political organizers who invested in the politics of the lot. The very presupposition of "we" and "us" is a minefield full of tensions and reckonings that "we" must come to terms with, as blood waters some lands without others. Yet these distinctions and hierarchizations do not bring us closer to social amalgamation. It is the recognition of difference as an inherent signifier of multiplicity and heterogeneous collectivity (outside of objectives for the production of value) that might lead us to form a deliberalized community despite neoliberal subject formation.It is the insistence on maintaining difference and the intentional perpetuation of tension, disagreement, and disappointment as a negative space within the social body that refuses homogeneity and hegemony. Still, many of us collectively rise in particular moments and in particular forms to create an event of political rupture, despite the precarity of political organizing infrastructures and the absence of a social body as such. How are we then collectively awakened? How do we find ourselves in the middle of a political event as a mass?

The simplistic, or rather, short answer is that our lives are shaped and saturated by violence; it is the escalation of this violence to extreme measures and *spectacular* manifestations that pushes us to the limit, where nothing but resistance and confrontation remain possible. Traditions of the past can show us how and why we rise and resist, but they also point to many socio-political awakenings that remained dormant, suspended in time, despite the presence of the structural conditions of total violence that anticipated the eruption of an uprising or a revolution. The reality of peoples who have endured, and those who continue to endure, extreme violence without ever arriving at the spark of collective mobilization, and the experience of others who have resisted, and those who continue to resist, in isolation and confinement, continues to pose a conundrum of whether to affirm or contest revolutionary eschatology.

However, between the moment of acknowledging the violence marked on the skin and subskin and that of collective action, there is a psycho-material process that facilitates a transformation. There are affective, embodied, and experiential assemblages that trigger, sublimate, or sustain such processes. If it isn't simply acts of speech that set social schemes in motion, uprisings, and revolutions from conspiring, then there must be something else, perhaps sensorial, that assembles the masses. It is aesthetics.

In his lifelong project to determine the grammar underpinning the interrelation between politics and aesthetics, Jacques Rancière formulates aesthetics as the regime that governs the "distribution of the sensible" or as "the system of a priori forms determining what presents itself to sense experience."[1] If, according to Rancière, politics are experiential—as in predicated on sensory experience before being rendered into thought, and in turn speech or action—where does this leave aesthetic form and aesthetics at large as the regime that governs the distribution of sensory experience itself through which politics come into being? Configuring aesthetic form through its delineating function, Rancière writes, "[aesthetics is] the delimitation of spaces and times, of the visible and the invisible, of speech and noise, that simultaneously determines the place and the stakes of politics as a form of experience. Politics revolves around what is seen and what can be said about it, around who has

1 Jacques Rancière, *The Politics of Aesthetics*. (United Kingdom: Bloomsbury Publishing, 2013), 13-14.

the ability to see and the talent to speak, around the properties of spaces and the possibilities of time." In this way, aesthetics inform political experience: Politics is not the social or political systems we have created for formal and informal assembly, governance, and organization. It is the sensory experiences inscribed in and through aesthetic form before they are rendered into thought, speech, or action. In this way, repression, expression, freedom, and bondage are conditions confined by the character of sensory experience, and the extent of the ability and *debility* to sense.[2]

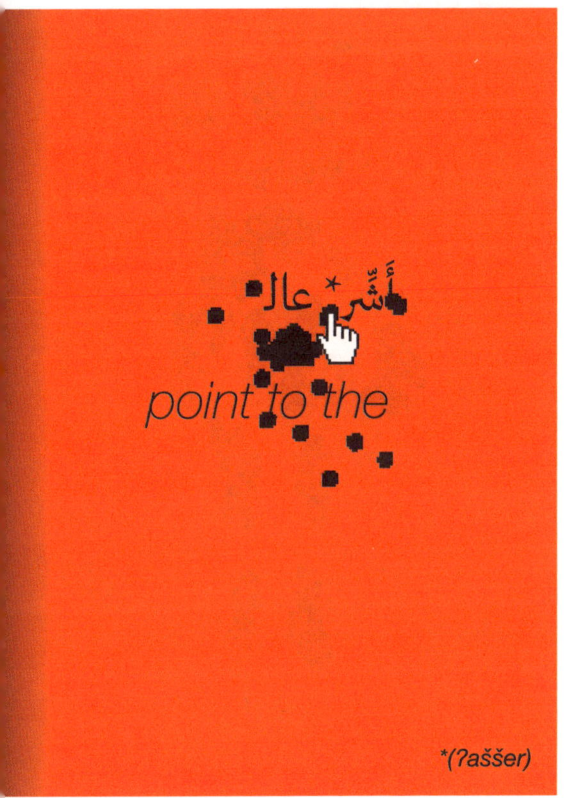

Political events for Rancière manifest exclusively within this aesthetic regime, via the production or assembling of ruptures in the reigning order of things. This means that political events do not occur dialectically in Rancière's regime of the sensible but through an assembling event that reveals an innate 'humanist' notion of equality that challenges the unevenly distributed participation in the aesthetic regime. In other words, Rancière's democratic aesthetics leave no room for negativity, as they do not conceive of a negative value within political form. In a political event à la Rancière, an oppressed or dehumanized individual or collective is ascended to being conceived and recognized as being equal to the oppressing group via

2
Jasbir Paur's theoretical intervention on the meaning of debility is significant here. Puar writes about debility as a biopolitical category used alongside disability and capacity, at once exposing their conceptual and historical limits and illucidating their interdependence. She argues that debility is a bodily configuration occurring through capitalist and repressive political violence effectively designating the terms of one's-body's participation and exclusion in the social and political. Debility as such becomes interesting as a literal and metaphorical injury to the body that deforms and limits one's sensory experience (indeed one's sensory ability), and therefore one's participation in the aesthetic regime—debility as the incapacitation to sense, debility as an enabler of "some forms of living and inhibit[or of] others. See: Jasbir K. Puar, *The Right to Maim: Debility, Capacity, Disability*. Durham: Duke University Press, 2017. Preface xiv-xxi.

an aesthetic configuration. The formulated transformation that occurs within this particular political moment is non-dialectical in the sense that the oppressed and the oppressor—the taxed and the benefactor—do not transform through a relationship that affects them both, but through the latter's recognition of the former's equality to himself. This recognition of equality is the recognition of equal sensory ability common to both the oppressor and oppressed, which up until that moment of rupture is governed unevenly by the dominant regime's tyranny. In short, despite the presupposed commonality in sensory ability and knowledge, there is a hierarchy of participation in sensory experience, and it is the rupture of this hierarchy that is envisioned as political.

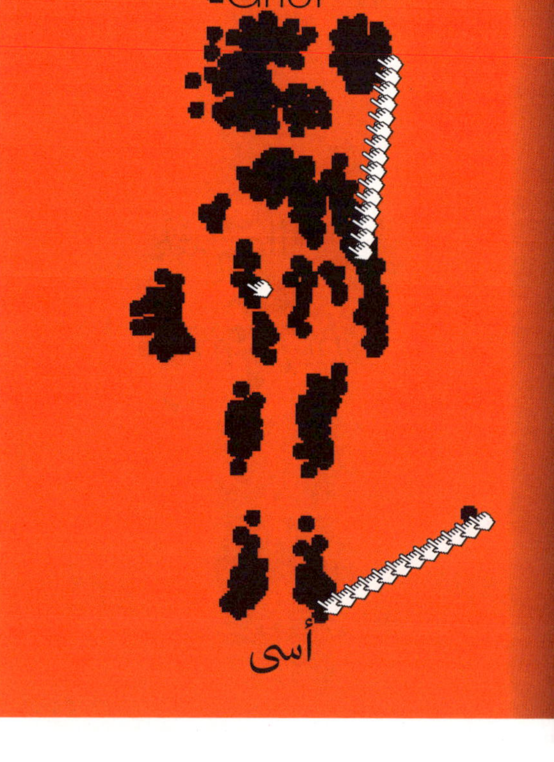

In the violent political contexts that oversaturate our experiences, persisting in extracting our futures—from colonization, displacement, genocide, enslavement, and incarceration—these notions of equality are weakening and losing any radical valence they claim to promise. Democratic notions of equality and their taxonomizing procedures offer limited space for political action at best, and at worst they nullify politics with their abstracting and emptying tendencies, and more often than not, conceal imperial, capitalist, and patriarchal objectives. These democratic notions of equality when effective (and transcendental according to their own social Darwinist logic), operate through forms of repressive assimilation: the inclusion of what is unequal occurs via its naturalization, itself an act of elimination of the negative. For to become supposedly equal one has to shed all that is undesired, unwanted, and uncaptured—the tensions and the splits of a subjectivity that refuses acculturation. These forms of democratic equalization seek to sever the negative to then subsume and devour it into the positive. They cause further fissures in subjugated subjectivities so they can become homogenized and plugged into the repressive structures that produce the splits. Deformed, disfigured, maimed—colonized, racialized, and exploited bodies—the dispossessed who seek equality to those who dictate the system of who is equal to them and who isn't, invoke the grotesque in liberal democracy.

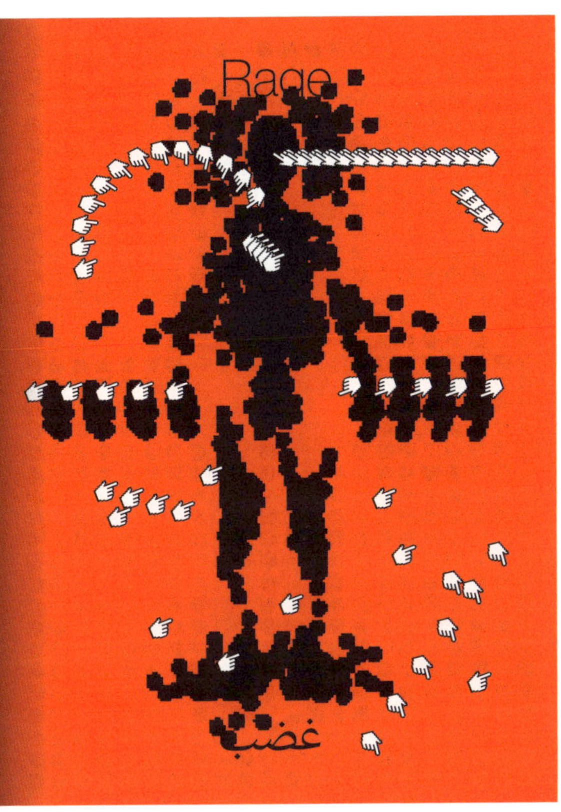

Writing from the very material and psychic reality of Palestine, and the political experiences birthed from the struggle for the liberation of subjects and objects, the living and the dead[3], there is an urgency to seriously ask: what of aesthetics exceeding notions of equality? Or more precisely, what of aesthetics beyond and outside of positivity, proletarian aesthetics labored in striking, revolting, and resisting, aesthetics that come into being despite prohibition? What of the aesthetics of negativity, aesthetics in the negative? These questions beg us to think dialectically and within unorthodox philosophical and political traditions. Artists Basel Abbas & Ruanne Abou-Rahme theorize a politics of "being in the negative" through an a-disciplinary artistic practice unfolding at the disjunction of sound, image, poetry, and performance. Thinking negativity as the domain of politics, not the transition from negativity (or any

3
Suhad Daher-Nashif has written extensively about how Israel holds the copses of Palestinians captive as a policy that began with the founding of the colony. Whether detained or imprisoned, Palestinians who were/are withheld in Zionist prisons remain there as hostages, even after their death. Daher-Nashef illucidates how the Israeli settler-colonial state uses policy this as a tactic to break apart Palestinian collectivity and as a form to have lasting damaging effects on Palestinian political subjectivies and psyche. See: Suhad Daher-Nashif, "Colonial Management of Death: To Be or Not to Be Dead in Palestine." *Current Sociology* 69, no. 7 (August 28, 2020): 945–62. https://doi.org/10.1177/0011392120948923.

conceptual equivalent[4]) into positivity (Rancière) nor the damning of negativity as the exclusion from politics where it only testifies against positivity (Adorno[5]), Abbas and Abou-Rahme conceive of the negative as a space-time of novelty and possibility that they insist on inhabiting, an experience akin to "breathing where you should not be able to breathe."[6] The truth of such aesthetics of the negative beckoned forth by Abbas and Abou-Rahme and materialized in their contemporary works of art speaks of the concrete materiality of Palestinian labor extracted, exploited, subjugated, "in debt. . . in the lack."[7] It speaks affectively of the material presence denied and negated, not as a quantitative or forensic plea, but a call for awakening and activation of a repressed and dormant political subjectivity.[8] To think politics and aesthetics through the negative, to be "the negative"—to perform, create, speculate, fabulate, imagine, and produce negatively—means to both formulate a way of being that is fully immersed and embedded in a struggle while assembling possibilities of living, imagining, and producing sensory social experiences and "an unusual and unprecedented knowledge"[9] through exclusion and in spite of it, slipping out of the cracks that fracture the regime of recognizability.[10]

If Abbas and Abou-Rahme are theorists of the negative, Jean Baudrillard would be the theorist of the positive. Writing two years before his death, in a time of his absolute disillusionment with political movements and radical critique, Baudrillard gives an emphatic account of contemporary society defined by power's total positivity: the complete obliteration of the work of the negative. The negative, for him, has been devoured and diminished. Its appearance through forms of political organizing and radical critique is an irony, a specter. Baudrillard describes the relation between the positive

4
Rancière works through the category of dissensus, or 'disagreement' which is the production of cracks and disruptions in the reigning regime governing the presentation and formalization of sensible experience, and the very distribution of the sensible. Dissensus makes clear the disparities between sensory experiences in a group. See: Jacques Rancière, *Dissensus: On Politics and Aesthetics*. (India: Bloomsbury Academic, 2010).

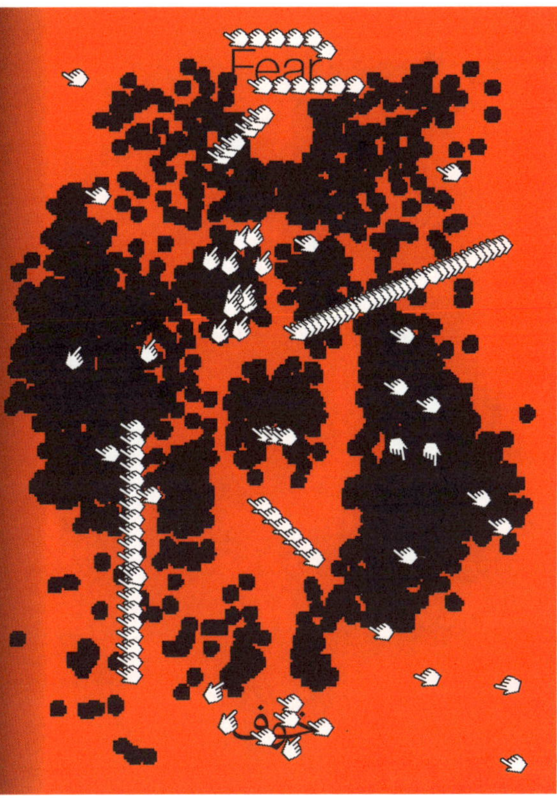

5
Adorno's negative dialectics function as an everlasting indictment of the positive. The positive according to Adorno, is what eliminates detail, particularity, and subjectivity through abstraction and assimilation. Capitalism in this sense is a system of positivity that subsumes everything. The Negative in turn is what testifies against this reality through detail and critique of the structure. However, Adornian dialectics are ossified, disinterested in bringing about a resolution, nor a dissolution of the dialectical schema. See: Theodor Adorno, *Negative Dialectics*. (United Kingdom: Taylor & Francis, 2003).

6
Basel Abbas and Ruanne Abou-Rahme, *May amnesia never kiss us on the mouth*, 2021–, https://mayamnesia.com.

7
Abbas and Abou-Rahme, *May amnesia*.

8
Abbas and Abou-Rahme, *May amnesia*.

9
Edward W. Said, and Jean Mohr. *After the last sky: Palestinian lives*. New York: Pantheon Books, 1986. 159. "Thus our need for a new consciousness [...] is that of a people whose national experience [... is] at those terrifying frontiers where the existence and disappearance of peoples fade into each other, where resistance is a necessity, but where there is also sometimes a growing realization to the need for an unusual and, to some degree, an unprecedented knowledge."

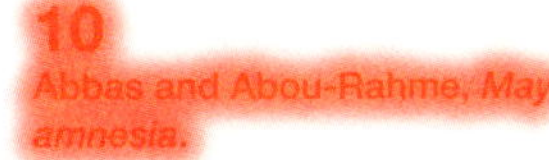

and the negative, in contemporary times of neoliberalism—the times of the reign of values and simulacra—as a "dialectical catastrophe."[11] These unambiguous statements are proffered through his analysis of the transition of power from *domination* into *hegemony*—the critical passage of postwar capitalism from the phase of production to the phase of consumption. If Baudrillard were alive he would claim that we are all complicit. Here, the dialectics between the master and the slave, the "historical work of critical thought, the relationship of forces against oppression, radical subjectivity against alienation are all (virtually) in the past."[12] Where would a social formation as such leave the work of the negative in the thought of Abbas and Abou-Rahme? The answer is rather simple: in everyday practices that insist, despite all threats of annihilation or attempts at assimilation, on producing labor uncaptured, a language misunderstood, and a form of being in the negative, *becoming the negative*, becoming unbound and resisting through forms of refusal in the position where no further loss remains possible.[13]

11
Jean Baudrillard, *The agony of power*. (South Pasadena, CA: Semiotext(e), 2010), 61.

12
Jean Baudrillard, *The agony of power*. (South Pasadena, CA: Semiotext(e), 2010), 60.

13
Basel Abbas and Ruanne Abou-Rahme, *Being the negative*, (New York/Palestine: Bilna'es, 2024). 5.

1

الصورة
Images
١

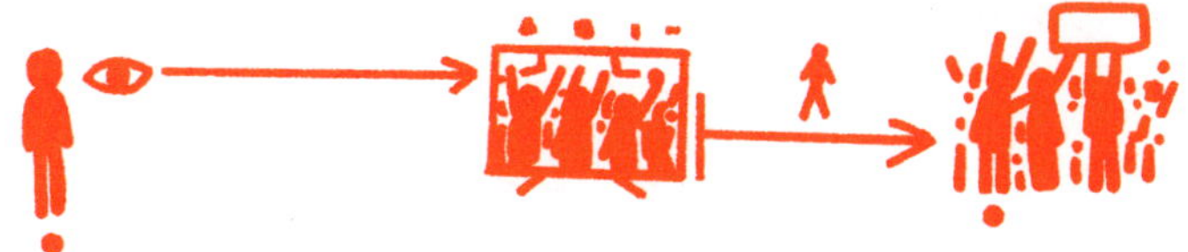

The daguerreotype process introduced in France in 1839 is agreed upon as the earliest recorded commercially viable photographic process. In the same year in Jerusalem, the first photograph taken in Palestine with that specific photographic process was recorded. While it is a striking fact, the overlap alludes to the various political, technosocial, and economic changes unfolding and forming in Palestine at the time (and in the years to follow) and their relation to how Palestine and its natives, the Palestinians, had begun to be captured within a new visual regime.

Though preceding (and certainly exceeding) the daguerreotype method, Palestine as *Holy Land* was already the subject of earlier methods of non-photographic reproduction—cultural demand a priori which configure technology. Colonial photographs of Palestine's wildlife and sacred architecture were summoned as objects that satisfy messianic fantasies. Scenic imagery of barren hills and fields signaled, to Europe, invitations for settlement and 'fertilization.' Documentation of Palestinian life served as a futuristic phantasm for the colonial life that *could be* established *there*. Aerial footage of villages, forests, and bodies of water was extracted to provide an aesthetic supply of data for the British and Zionists, a visual basis for settlement, administration, border-making, militarization, and population management. Portraiture of the native subject indeed produced colonized subjectivities across colonial terrains of exoticization, racialization, surveillance, and informationalization. These were all apparatuses in formation, that either informed photographic development or were informed by the visual regime beckoned by photography.

1

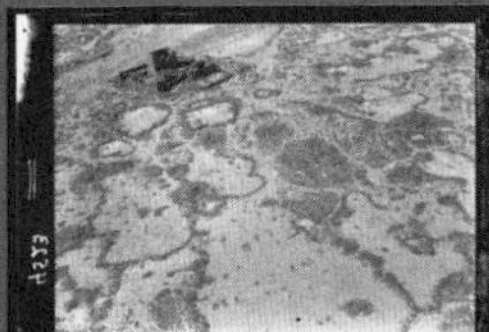
LC-DIG-matpc-15956

2

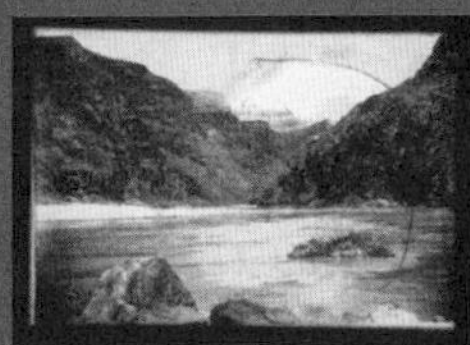
LC-DIG-matpc-15044

3

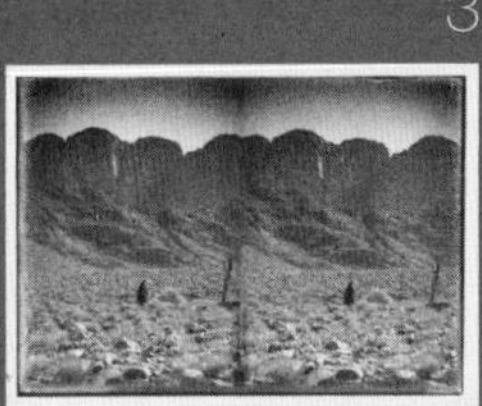
LC-DIG-matpc-02011

4

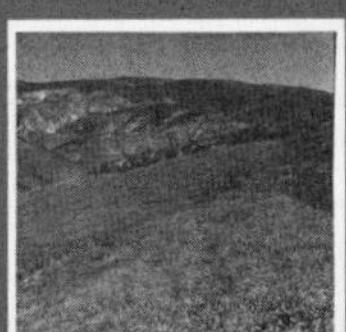
LC-DIG-matpc-15050

1	و
2	ج.هـ.ف.ر
3	ح.ص.ش
4	أ.ب.ل.ع
5	د.ز.ط.ي.ق.م.س.ك.ت

5

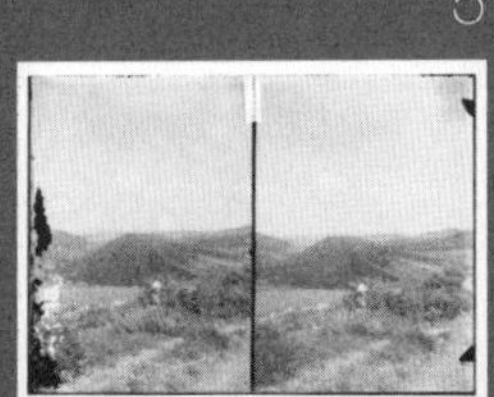
LC-DIG-matpc-10574

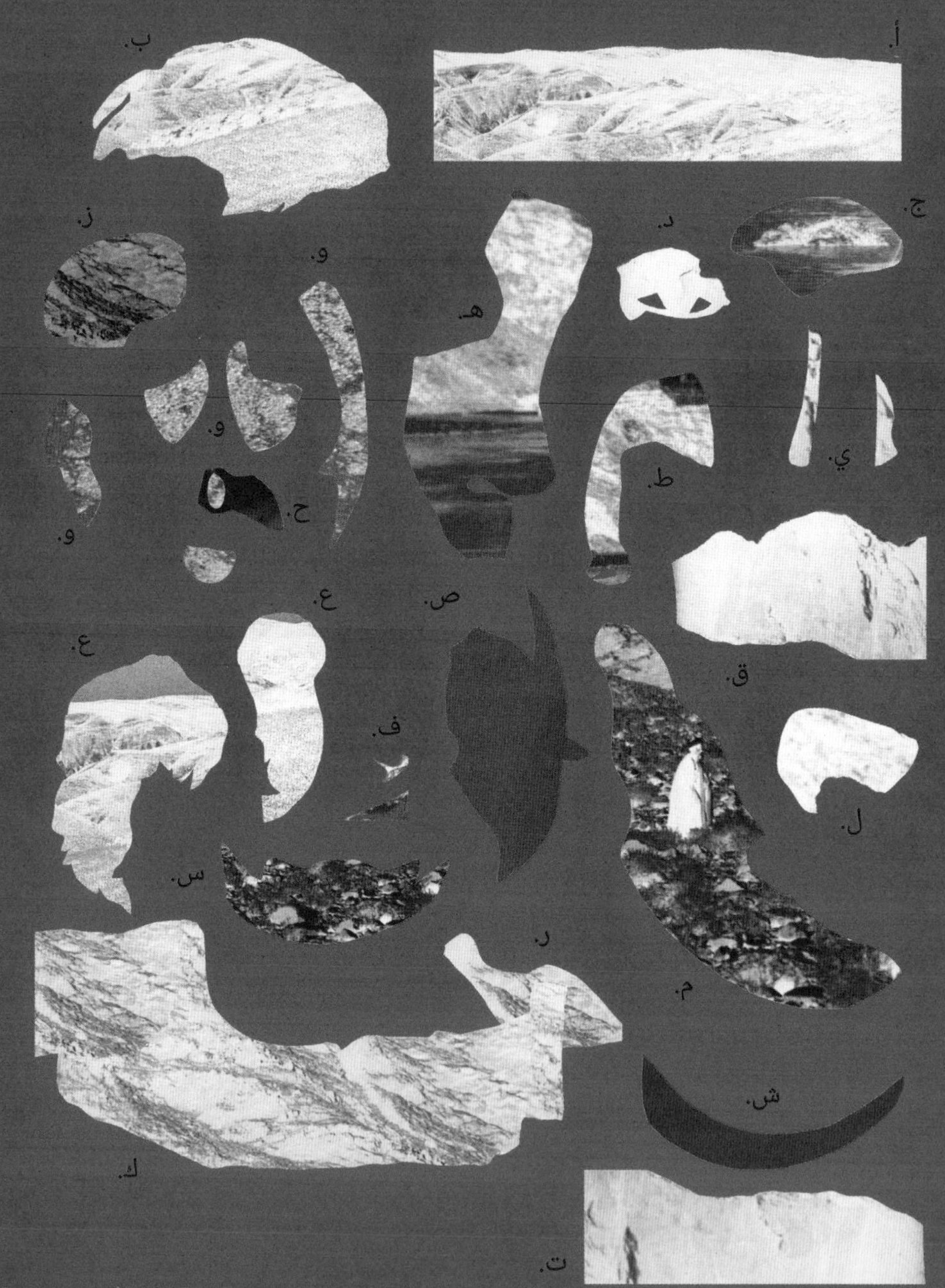

أ.
ب.
ج.
د.
ز.
و.
هـ.
و.
ي.
ط.
ح.
و.
ص.
ع.
ع.
ق.
ف.
ل.
س.
ر.
م.
ش.
ك.
ت.

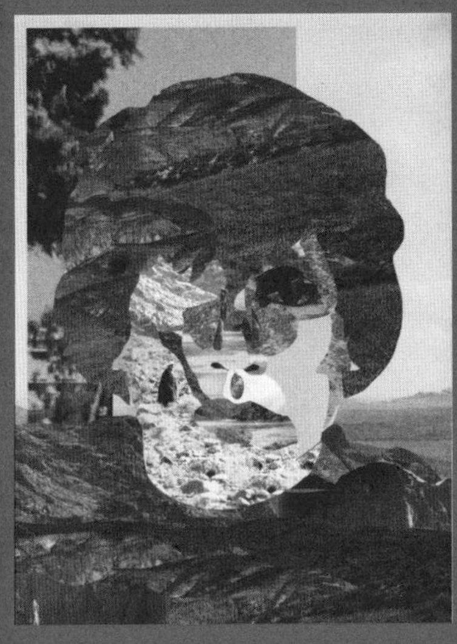

What, then, do we do with images that capture us? Do we burn them ceremonially in an act of collective exodus from a tyrant visual regime? If we set them ablaze, will we also be burned? If we could terminate these images, what would it mean to be one without an image? Once captured, can we escape? Can we slip out, and if so, what is at stake? One can seize this opportunity to recite and rehearse the colonial, racializing, and capitalist violence of the image, but many thinkers have done so tirelessly and in ways unnecessary to exceed. The arrival of photography and indeed modernity in Palestine, whether enforced by British and Zionist colonization or cultivated by the Arab bourgeoisie of the 19th and 20th centuries introduced the advent of new technological, social, and subjectivizing forms of coercion and domination. Nevertheless, they have also produced political forms of being and participation within modernity and its restructurings. That is the work of the negative in political subjectivities: to formulate unprecedented political tactics, strategies, and modern ways of life. To produce, with the same modern technologies, sensory political experiences that open up alternative temporal realities. As subjects of colonial modernity, Palestinians continue to maneuver, mutate, and produce new ways of living and being despite these regimes of violence, constantly shapeshifting in search of life in dying.

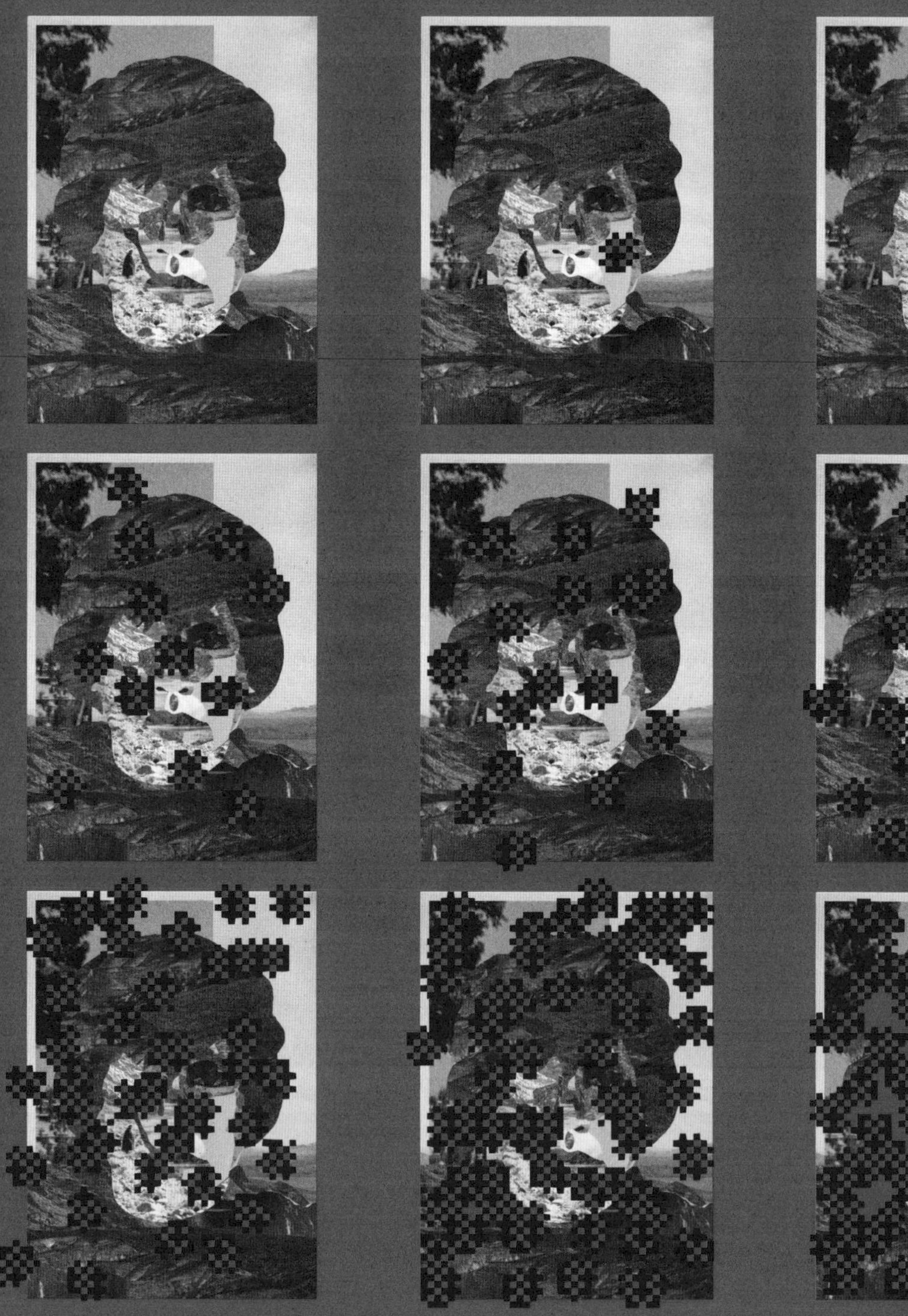

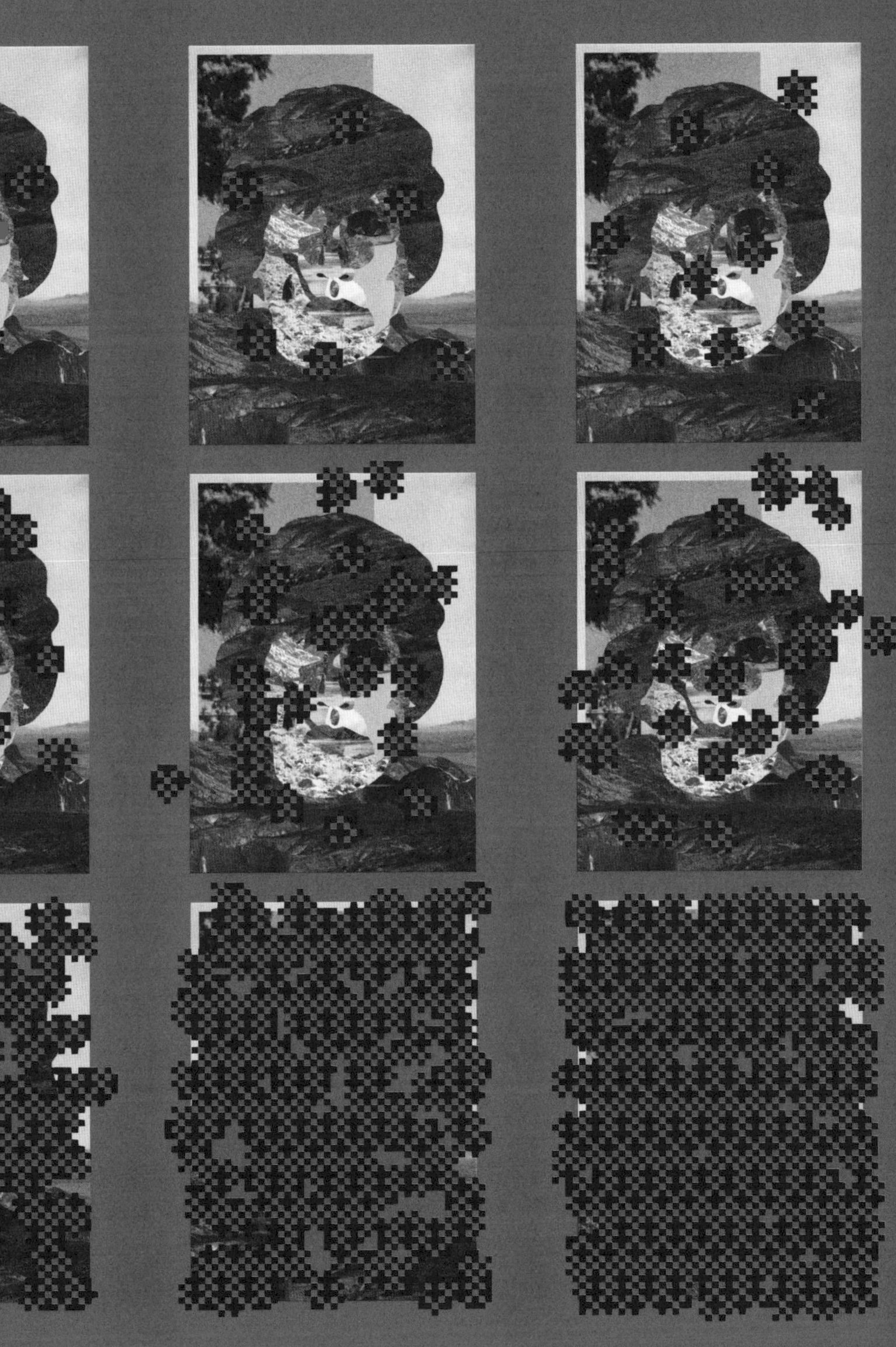

Desiring Images

أريد أن اكون تلك الصورة

During the national Palestinian uprising of May 2021, we were under the spell of images. It was unclear whether these images were trying to capture us as we revolted, or whether we were trying to capture them as they fled. For months, particular images dominated our field of vision. The virtual realm occupied our psychic investments through immaterial images. They became imprinted in our Imaginary, initiating new meanings in our system of signification, articulating new signifiers of what is possible, what reality a certain image could signify, and how the signification of such an imagined reality testifies to its materiality.[14] These images avow the potential reality a certain image could conjure even if fleetingly, and reveal how this conjuring of *what could be possible* turns these immaterial images into a material force in our lives. Like thought-images, the images that circulated online were digital and immaterial, allowing us to project on them the Palestine we wanted to see, while also leaving a trace of how this sought-after Palestine unfolded within them. Like an apparition, a future ghost, and a premonition, they lured us into the worlds that they allowed us to make open, initiating new openings in the field of vision, and cracking a possibility within what was once impossible.[15] We repeatedly watched images of settlers invading the homes of Palestinians in Jerusalem, Jaffa, and Masafer Yatta as spectacles of our ongoing displacement. The struggle is national, but Palestine's colonial reality isolates these

14
Émile Benveniste, *Problems in General Linguistics*. (United States: University of Miami Press, 1971), 45.

15
Writing about Emile Benveniste's critique of Saussurian linguistics, Mona Benyamin writes how in Arabic, "the word for imagination [image-imagine-im-agination] is khayal, stemming from the root verb khāla [past tense; "thought"], and defined by the Lexicon of Modern Arabic as "a lasting image in the soul following the absence of the tangible, a personal image that illustrates an abstract meaning clearly" and is also synonymous with the words "ghost" and "shadow." . . . khayal is founded on the root verb 'thought' and therefore inseparable from it, and as Benveniste tells us "thought is not matter to which language lends form, since at no time could this 'container' be imagined as empty of its contents, nor the 'contents' as independent of their 'container'". Thank you Mona Benyamin for sharing your unpublished draft with me. Thank you Nour Annan for challenging my argument through the relation between thought-images and digital images.

centers of confrontation, making them appear sporadic, each locale a persuasive microcosm swaying us to believe that the violence of the settler colony *here* or *there* is exceptionally mismatched with the rest of the land—but only if we let it. Under this colonial tactic of fragmentations, images of repressive violence granted us exclusive access to Palestine's multitudes, allowing us to bypass the settler cartography, even if virtually. And for a moment in May '21, those same images were overpowered by others of a different nature: images of families dispossessed from Masafer Yatta were momentarily replaced with images of settlers leaving our villages, cities, and towns that they had named as theirs. Streets pictured and imagined as ones constructed only for Jews, suddenly visualized the return of the repressed presence of Palestinians, running in spaces they are not allowed to be. Images of Akka's old neighborhoods turned into seaside Israeli suburbs, unfolded on our screens as spaces to be reclaimed from the grips of settlement and colonial property.

In Al-Lydd, we saw images of Israelis evacuating historical Palestinian homes turned Israeli property. At the same time, Palestinians were setting tires ablaze, blocking roads and highways to prevent settlers from reaching them, perhaps in an attempt to liberate the land from colonial confinement and possession. Observing these scenes virtually across Palestine, these images projected a liberated present horizon that was visible from within the same colonized lands we inhabited. One particular image persisted. It was captioned "Al-Lydd is now free. May 11th, 2021, is Al-Lydd's Day of Independence. [...] They wanted to occupy a neighborhood; we liberated an entire city." This image wasn't like other images. It was different in the capacities it held. There was something libidinal about it, the way it was labored, performed, then circulated. Despite its proliferation on social media(tion) platforms saturated by the reign of capital's positivity, the image maintained a fleeting negativity that defied capture. What it offered its viewers negated the logic of consumption. That image was of a masked man who had climbed to the top of a street light column while holding the flag of Palestine, sticking it through the

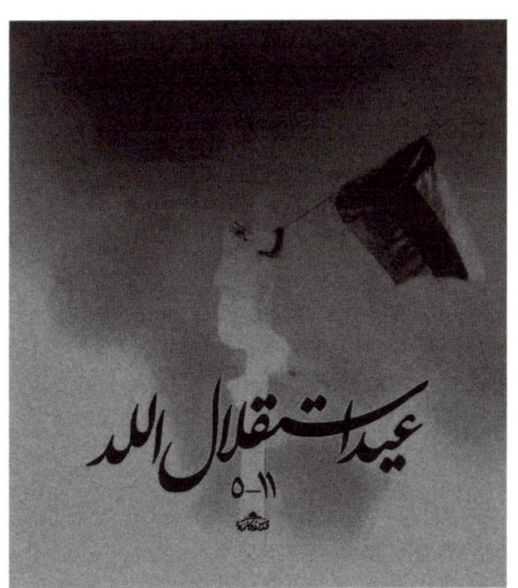

cracks he had punctured in an act of defiance. After the scene was captured, someone had stamped it with Arabic calligraphy that read: *"Al-Lydd's Day of Independence. May 11th."* Since it appeared online, it began to disseminate quickly. We didn't know if we believed it or not, but the possibility it portrayed allowed us to bypass the limitations of our colonial condition. What this image signaled was a call from a parallel time.[16] Regardless of the scene itself, whether Al-Lydd was in fact liberated or not, it materialized a collective revolutionary imaginary in massly disseminated aesthetic form. The image materialized a possibility suspended in a distant awaited time as an embodied event of the present. The masked man performed an act of rebellion with his body, this act was then captured, and the raw image was edited and circulated to communicate a new reality, between fantasy and concrete fulfillment, of Palestinian liberation. This libidinal image reached us and activated us. "If Al-Lydd declared its independence, what stops Ein Qinya, Rafah, Haifa, or Jenin from declaring theirs?" was a question that persisted in our minds and on our tongues. What if we were the masked man, what if his performance was ours, what if we did what he did?

"Political Mimesis" is the term used by Jane Gaines to describe the relationship between spectators of documentary footage of political revolt, and the bodies captured in that footage performing political acts. She writes, "[...] political mimicry has to do with the production of affect in and through the conventionalized imagery of struggle: bloodied bodies, marching throngs, angry police. But clearly such imagery will have no resonance without politics, the politics that has been theorized as consciousness, in Marxism as class consciousness...The dilemma here is that whereas we would never want to suggest that the process of developing class consciousness is involuntary or imitative, we need to concede that in the thrall of group song, in the heat of battle, in bodily strain and physical resistance, certainly, there could sometimes be an aspect of the involuntary, an aspect that 'kicks in' on top of politicized consciousness." Although Gaines' question examines the capacity of documentary filmmaking to instigate political change, or at the least, political awakening which is in itself a transformation from one state to another, the query persists in our contemporary reality that is saturated by images of struggle unfolding on our screens in real-time. There is indeed a difference between the revolutionary documentary image and the documented image captured in the time of revolution, but that difference has to do with the economies of circulation, and materiality of production, or said differently, the aesthetics and politics of images and the aestheticization of political imagery.[17]

The framework of mimesis proposed by Gaines for understanding the politics of collective consciousness facilitated through images is compelling for two reasons. The first is that in the age of reproduction, mimesis offers a resolution of multiplication beyond notions of capitalist production. In capitalism, desires are produced and reproduced for consumption and implicit subjugation. We want to buy what others buy, consume what others consume, and perform exploited labor to be desired as others are desired. Mimesis is desire imitating the desires of others—not desire reproduced, which means its form is empty of content. In the case of "political mimesis" per Gaines, it is desire imitating the subversive desires of others. Despite the emptiness, the hollow form of that desire, the form remains dangerous and antagonistic to the order of power. Mimesis in moments of political upheaval offers an immediate linkage between aesthetics and psychosocial experience. This relation between the spectating body's desire to perform an act similar to the body captured in the image deserves examination and scrutiny.

The prominent historical psychoanalytic interpretation of art, or of aesthetic form occurring in the subject of psychoanalysis is understood through sublimation, providing the "drive" as Lacan has put it, with a "satisfaction different from its aim."[18] Sublimation in art is, in its essence, an operation that produces value between objects of desire—a value that cannot be exchanged, one without a function per capitalist logic of exchange. When we go back to the notion of

16
Walid Daqqah, "Domination with Time," *Awan*, June 16, 2021 https://www.awanmedia.net/article/6046.

17
Mary Jirmanus Saba, "What's the Use of a Strike Archive?" *Critical Times* 5, no. 3 (December 1, 2022): 663–87. https://doi.org/10.1215/26410478-10030274.

18→

political mimicry, this imaginary psychic relationship between the spectating body and the body performing political acts, a meta-relationship of values is formed. The value of the sublimated desire materialized in aesthetic form and embodied by the performing body in the image forms a relationship with a new value produced by a sublimated desire materializing in political mimicry. Since both of these values are forms without content, they have the capacity to be purposed for revolutionary political objectives. The repressed therefore are able to use imagery, circulating on social media platforms, produced with technosocial regimes of surveillance and identification for the purposes of capitalist accumulation and political suppression, and repurpose them for political ends that go against the very conditions of their production.

This observation isn't merely a sensorial experience rendered into intellectual abstraction, as activists, artists, and others who find themselves in the heart of a political event without prior planning have continuously offered reflections that attest to this psychic experience. One well-circulated account was published under the alias "L" on the leftist feminist Iranian platform by the collective

18
In Lacan's most developed formulation of sublimation, it is defined as an operation that involves the three registers of the unconscious: the Imaginary, the Symbolic, and the Real. He writes, "The sublimation that provides the Trieb with a satisfaction different from its aim—an aim that is still defined as its natural aim—is precisely that which reveals the true nature of the Trieb insofar as it is not simply instinct, but has a relationship to das Ding as such, to the Thing insofar as it is distinct from the object." (Jacques Lacan, *The Ethics of Psychoanalysis, 1959-1960: The Seminar of Jacques Lacan, Book VII*. (United Kingdom: Routledge, 1999), 111). Lacan articulates it as the transcendence of the Imaginary object to the Real Thing via the Symbolic: "raising the object to the dignity of the Thing." (Jacques Lacan, *The Ethics of Psychoanalysis, 1959-1960: The Seminar of Jacques Lacan, Book VII*. (United Kingdom: Routledge, 1999), 112). In the case of the work of art, it is the image of the Real that can never be represented, yet invoked. The dignity of the "Thing" which is not the thing itself is that of sexual desire (Imaginary) elevated into aesthetic form (Real) configured through the symbolic.

19
The text was originally posted in Persian to harasswatch.com on Wednesday, September 28, 2022, and can be accessed online through this link:https://bit.ly/3AWsNk9. The first English translation by Alireza Doostdar with input from the author was published on Jadaliyya under the title "Figuring a Women's Revolution: Bodies Interacting with their Images" and can be accessed online through this link: https://bit.ly/3XCal3O.

20
L. "Figuring a Women's Revolution: Bodies Interacting with Their Images." Translated by Alireza Doostdar. *Jadaliyya*, October 5, 2022. https://bit.ly/3XCal3O.

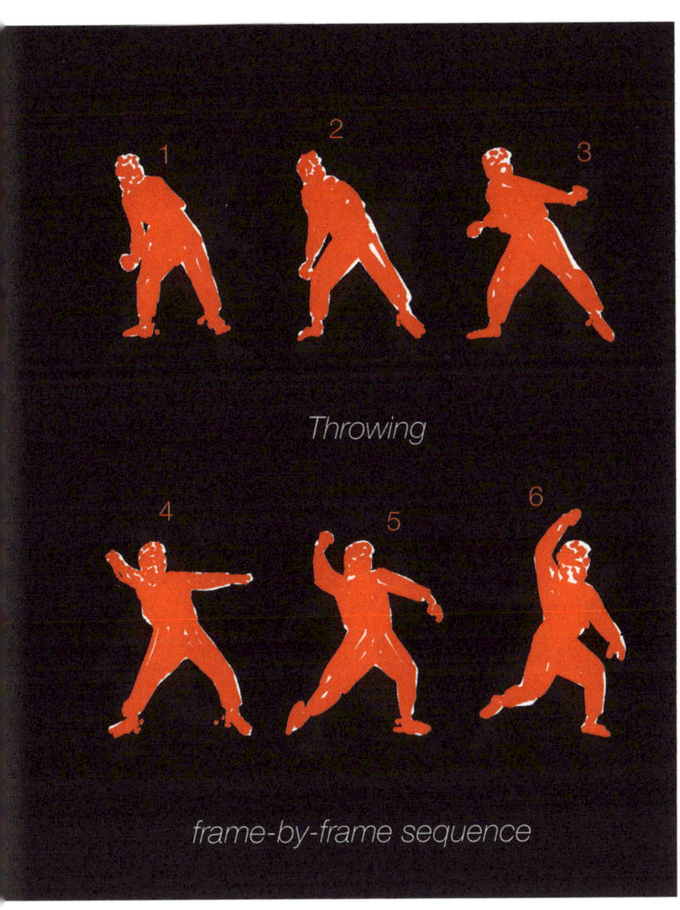

Harass Watch amidst the uprising of 2022 in Iran.[19] The essay is marked by what propelled its writing: "an attempt to understand an intuition born of experiencing a gap: A gap between viewing photos and videos of protests online, and presence in the street. [...] an effort to explicate the short-circuit that courses in the opening between these two domains—virtual space and the reality of the street—in this historic moment."[20] In 'Figuring a Women's Revolution: Bodies Interacting with their Images', L writes about her dual experience watching still and moving images of revolt, of bodies burning scarves, vandalizing state property, and being beaten, and that of her finding herself in the streets recreating the same scenes she had watched prior. Her account testifies to how a certain kind of knowing, or a dormant memory stored in the

21
Ernst Bloch, *The Heritage of Our Times*. Germany: Polity Press, 2015.

22
Ernst Bloch, "Nonsynchronism and the Obligation to Its Dialectics." Translated by Mark Ritter. *New German Critique*, no. 11 (1977): 22. https://doi.org/10.2307/487802.

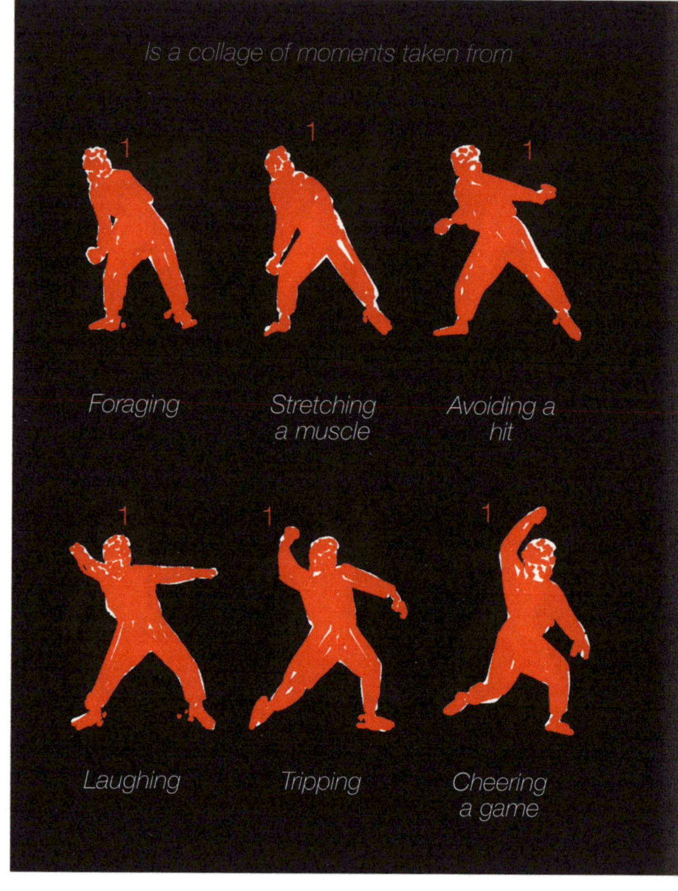

body, infors a reaction that moves quicker than one compelled by reason. Her account is striking because it articulates mimesis as an aesthetic form that evokes unconscious desires. She watches images of protests and revolt and finds herself recreating the scenes captured within them because of a desire to mimic them. L also contemplates how the time of revolution is when time opens up and temporalities clash. Our bodies move faster than us, and we rise always in a delay to a revolution reproduced time and again as one that is *awaited*.[21] This reflection is resonant with Ernst Bloch's note on the non-synchronous: "Not all people exist in the same Now. They do so only externally, by virtue of the fact that they may all be seen today. But that does not mean that they are living at the same time with others."[22] This begs a scrutinization of the psyche under such transformations and transactions.

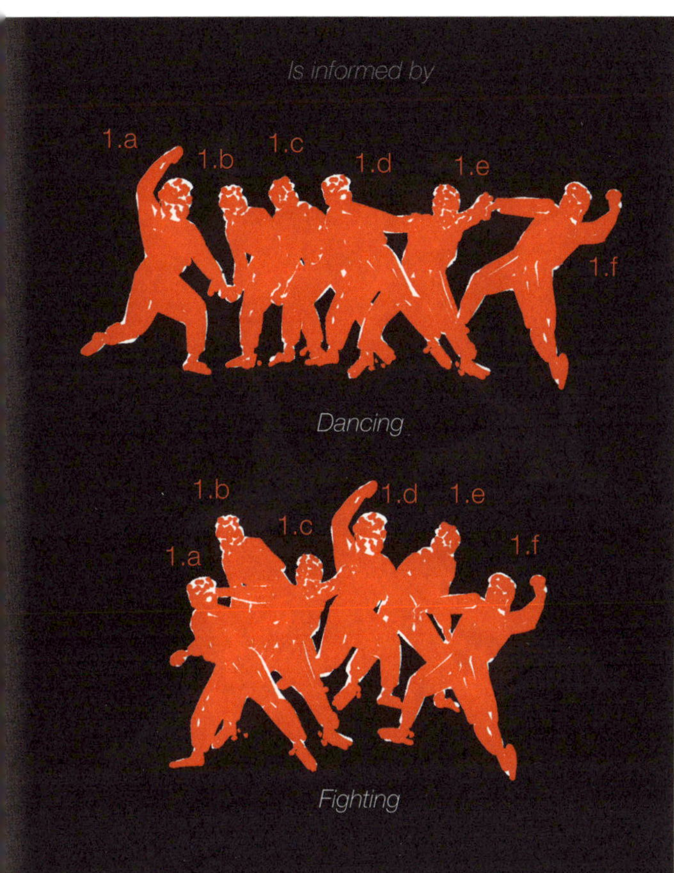

23 L., *Figuring a Women's Revolution*.

L writes, "The space between me and the images I had desired had grown very small. I myself was those images. I would suddenly see myself in a circle burning headscarves, as though we had always been burning scarves. [...] My body had unconsciously performed those things I had seen other protestors do. [...] The palpable difference between this protest and the protests I had experienced before was a passage from the 'movement of a crowd' to the 'creation of a situation.'"[23] This psychic experience is both facilitated and materialized through aesthetics, through the sensuous and the sensorial. L's account also attests to a particular paradoxical reality of political organizing in neoliberal times: the passage she speaks of from the "movement of a crowd" to the "creation of a situation" enunciates the reality of a liberalized and fragmented collective in a state of inability to organize itself as one mass.

24
Byung-Chul Han, *Psychopolitics: Neoliberalism and New Technologies of Power*. (United Kingdom: Verso Books, 2017).

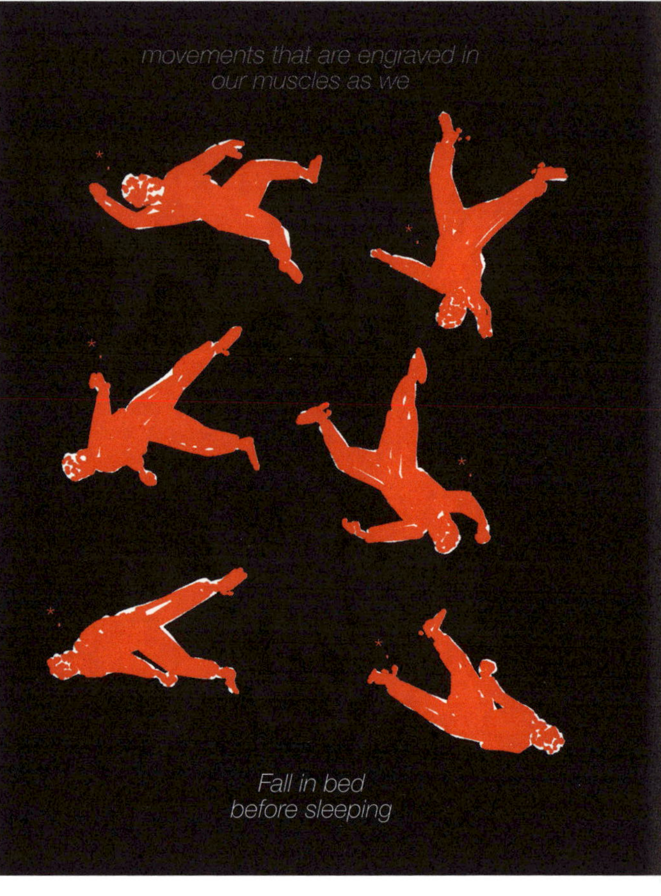

However, L's account also articulates how this collective finds itself almost involuntarily as a mass of individuals engaged in subversive political activity. Subjective desires are sedated and captured, held hostage by technosocial regimes of mediation, while at the same time, in a political moment, an unintentional mass is formed despite liberalization.[24] It is precisely the inherent quality of psychic desires defined by a "lack" and the objects of desire formed through alienation that offer us this radical opening. This opening manifests itself through the aesthetic regime, in this case, through the proliferation of political imagery of revolt, confrontation, and the transgression of boundaries previously deemed unsurpassable. L's account in 2022, read comparatively to that of Palestinians in 2021, accentuates the ways in which Palestinians have been engaged in aesthetic lineages of revolt that precede the contemporary colonial reality and its technologies.

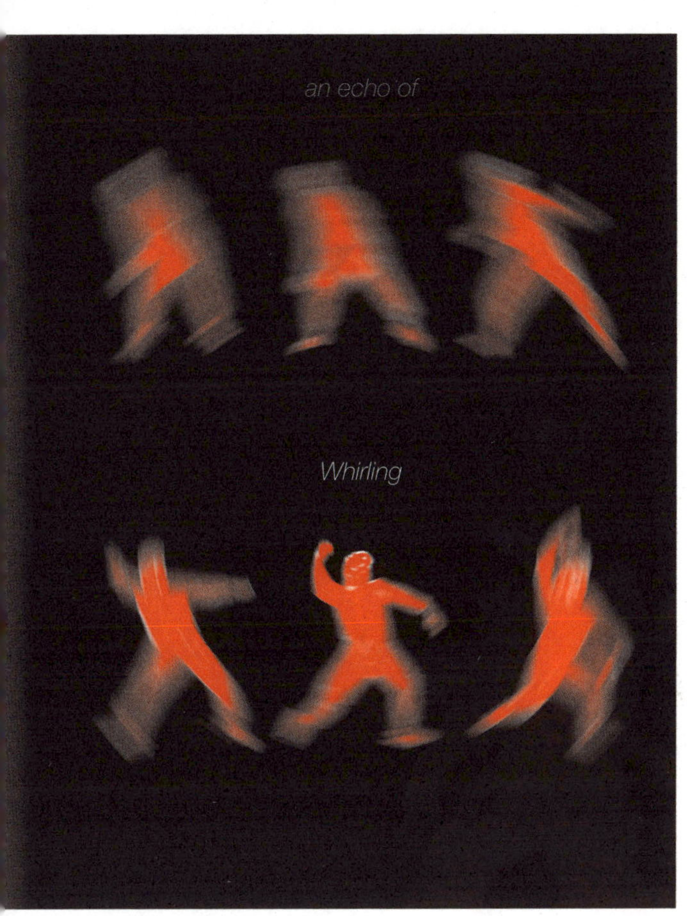
an echo of
Whirling

1(8)

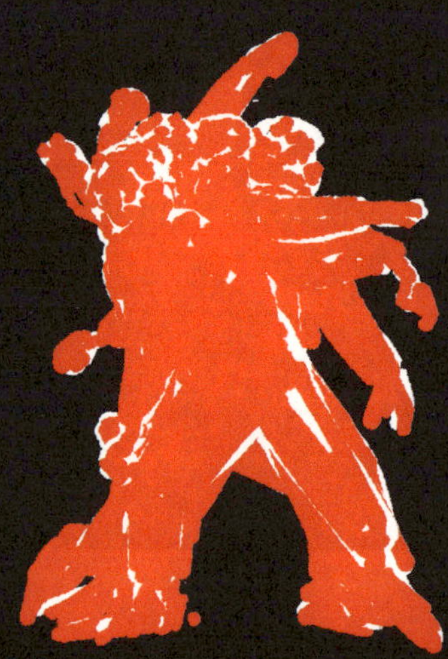

Throwing

frame-on-frame sequence

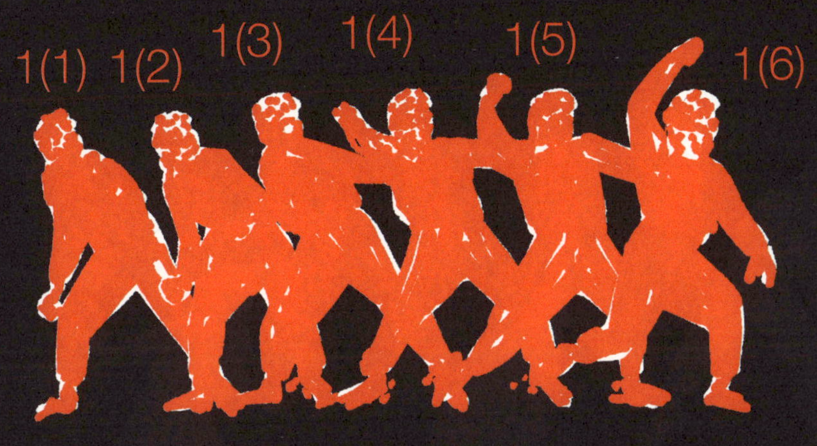

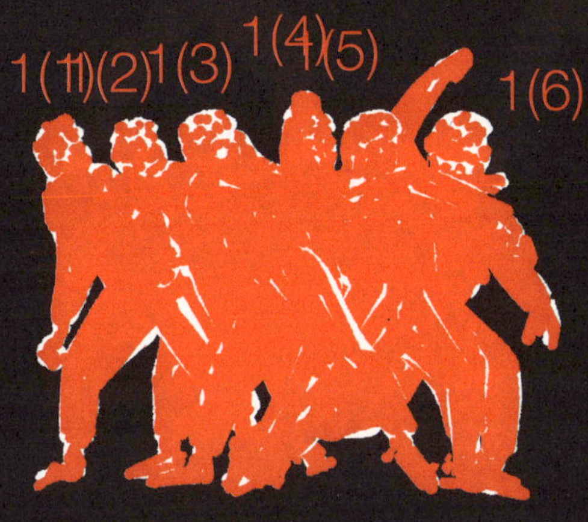

Frames

Vibrating

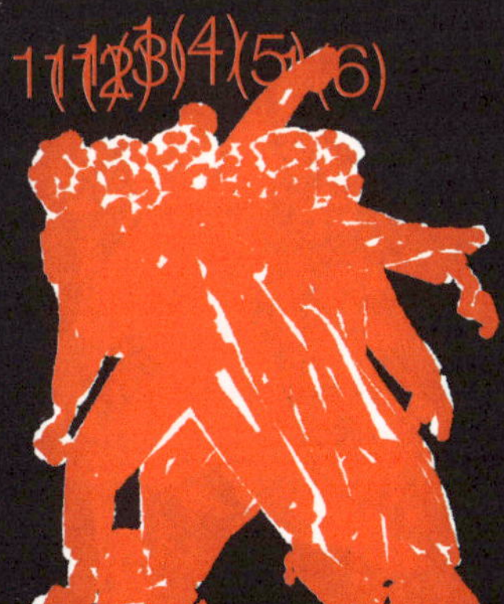

away

from

eachother

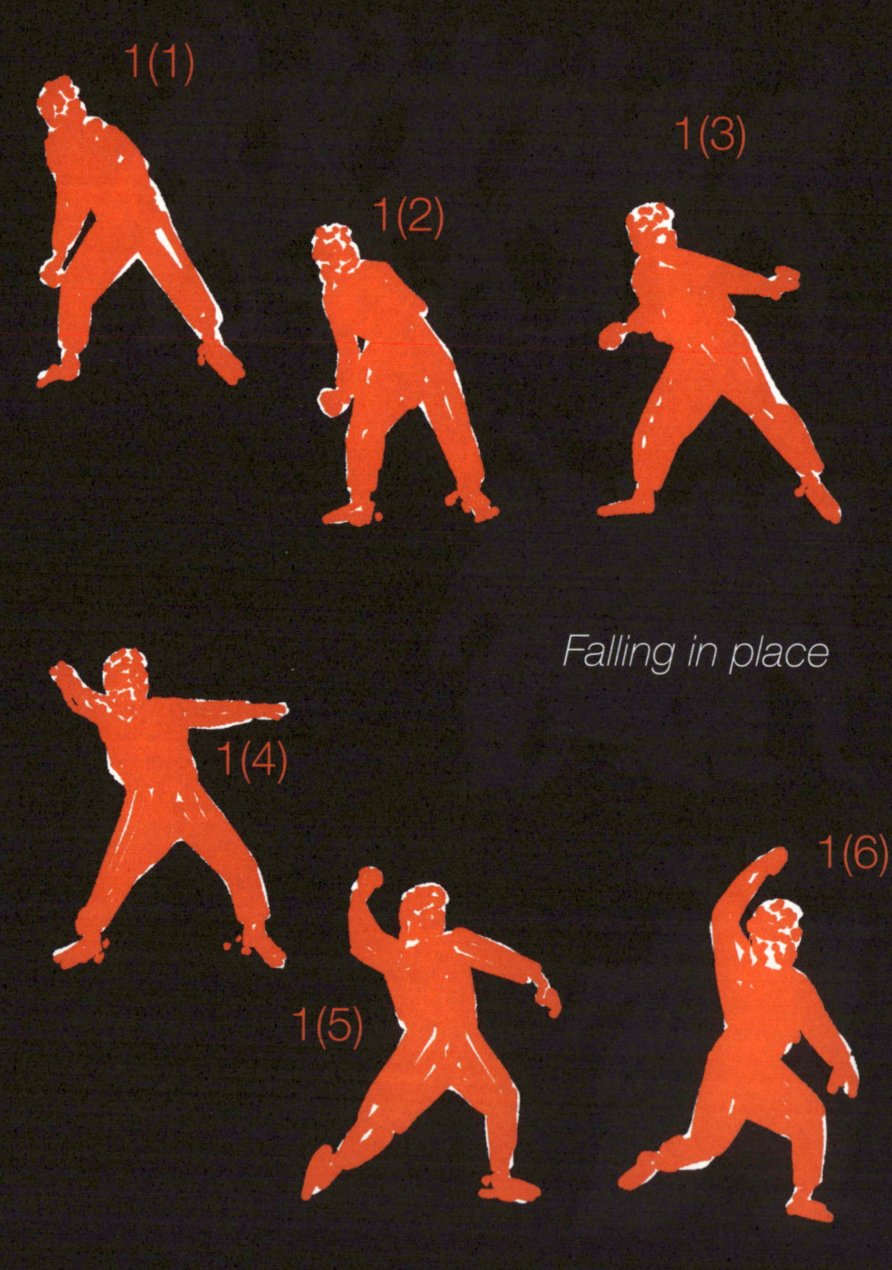

Falling in place

Through memories

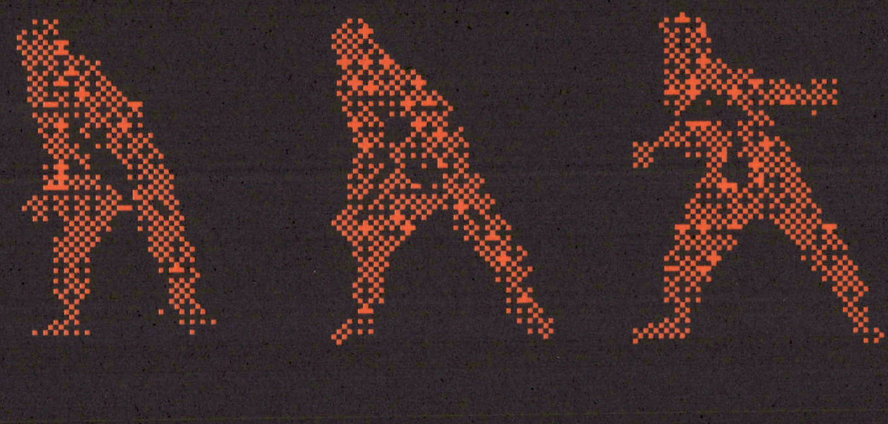

and screens

"Throwing" a frame

Did you think I was going to let you capture me this way?

Images in Palestine have a revolutionary logic of their own. One exceptional form of image-making birthed by struggle is that of Palestinians at the time of their detainment. Among these iconic historical images is that of the late Palestinian militant and political activist Fatima Bernawi on the day of her sentencing to life in prison. The capture occurred a few months after the Six-Day War, on October 10th, 1967. Two days prior, on October 8th, Cinema Zion in Jerusalem was set to screen a film that celebrated the war. Fatima Bernawi was living in Jerusalem at the time, and politically organizing with the Palestinian Liberation Organization. On that day, Fatima, with the assistance of her sister Ehsan, planted a bomb in the cinema house to protest the screening of the film and its successive celebrations. The operation was intercepted shortly after the bomb was discovered by a security guard and neutralized by Israeli officials, without it ever detonating. Ehsan managed to flee to Jordan immediately after the operation, but Fatima remained in Jerusalem, where she was taken into custody. Two days later, Fatima was sentenced to life in prison by the Israeli Authorities. While handcuffed, the Israeli judge asked her to stand still for a mugshot to be taken of her, to announce the news in the Hebrew newspapers. In an act of defiance, Bernawi stuck her tongue out, mocking the Israeli judge, his sham court of law, and the colonial state he represented.

Why would a militant woman such as Fatima Bernawi stick her tongue out in this manner? What is the purpose of such a gesture? What kind of images did Bernawi leave behind? In the court hearings, Bernawi had not once denied any allegation against her, nor did she portray a false image of who she was as someone embedded in the armed struggle for the liberation of her homeland. However, as an icon of Palestinian resistance, Fatima Bernawi's image is nothing like those of her contemporaries. Regardless of Bernawi's intentions, or unintentional impulses, she acted on a desire to subvert the image that was taken of her in a moment of supposed weakness and defeat. She was never photographed in militant clothing or holding her Klashinkov or other arms like, say, Leila Khaled. She instead proffers an unconventional image of militancy through the very precarity of her condition and the poverty of visual techniques available to her at the moment that her incarceration is announced. It is with her body and mischievous demeanor, not her arms or militant iconography, that she subverted an image that was supposed to represent a moment of defeat and captivity. Staring at the camera with a piercing stare and her tongue out, Bernawi challenged the purpose of the image captured by the Israelis, sabotaging it into one where she appears as a Palestinian who's defiant, playful, free.

The mugshot of Bernawi was published by Israeli officials in newspapers to demonstrate colonial might and conquest in eliminating a native threat. However, the image was hijacked shortly after by Palestinians who predominantly disseminated it as a totem of triumph and resilience. The repurposing of the image destabilized its material conditions, instrumentalizing it to fracture the condition of its very making, to fracture the colonial order of domination and oppression latent in the image. The image defined in its rectangular enclave was punctured by the subject it sought to capture, turning it from an image constructed for surveillance and symbolic defeat into one that signals the power of the repressed.

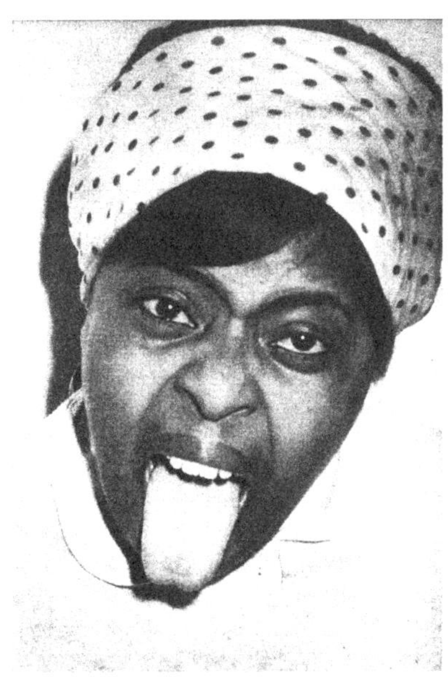

Despite the uniqueness of Bernawi's image, one could make connections between it and another lineage of images produced by Palestinians at the time of their captivity. This form of negatively-accumulating production of resistant aesthetics can also be understood through the logic of hijacking. It is as if such collective practices orchestrate a disruption to the designated trajectory of coercive colonial photography, fueled by the drive to dominate, surveil, and dehumanize. These disruptions lead the image astray from its intended destination and toward an alternative emancipatory one, reversing the process of capture. It is crucial to locate Bernawi's poorly equipped (though affective) effort to intervene with the image within a societal practice that goes beyond the cult iconography of her image. To clarify this link, we must go beyond a reading of images that operates exclusively at the representational level, and move into a formal analysis of aesthetic strategies deployed within Palestine's revolutionary tradition in their cooptation of colonial images and their rehabilitation into an anticolonial function. What exceptionalizes Bernawi's image is the conditions of its production and Bernawi's intuitive impulse in a moment of subjugation. Similar images of Palestinians smiling (sometimes with a victory sign if they are not yet handcuffed) are often taken at the moment of detainment. What had begun as an intuitive gesture during the First Intifada, had evolved into a common tactic by the Second Intifada. Palestinians across regions and ages, and despite colonial re-territorializations of Palestinian land, have been smiling to the camera at the moment of their arrest and subjection to Israeli police and military violence. We can see this, for example, when Jaser Dwaikat was detained on April 4, 2022, with a rifle pointed to his head by an Israeli soldier in Za'atara, or Odai Maswada who was attacked and taken to a prison cell at Damascus gate in Jerusalem that same day, or Mohammed Fakhuri on June 1, 2021, or Zeina Halawani when she was at the police station two days before that, or Ronny Shaheen from Tarshiha smiling with a soldier's foot on his head during the 2014 protests against Israeli's Prawer Plan.[25]

This simple gesture, performed as a subversive visual tactic, is an impoverished yet very powerful form of image-making. The gestures infiltrate and intervene either at the level of authorship (who captures the image ceases to hold the power of its narrative), altering the representational paradigm of the subject and the event of the photograph when arrested by Israelis. Often these gestures of smiling despite captivity, perform a signal of sorts, sending a call to comrades and kin. The settler colonial reality in neoliberal times renders the mere act of convening collectively impossible, often illegal. Given these repressive conditions, it is astounding to observe how such visual tactics find their way into becoming part of an anticolonial lexicon and language shared across Palestine. Especially when we reckon with how these tactics have neither been announced to be followed or replicated by any existing leadership, nor collectively concurred at any tier of political organizing, but intuitively and organically mimicked. What emerges is a revolutionary tradition embedded in an aesthetic philosophy of resistance, one birthed from the streets—a theory of the proletariat.

The act of smiling, performing embodied victory, of acting unperturbed in moments of captivity and spectacular violence, has become so commonplace by now that many detainees are asked to smile when their kin capture their image. When prisoners are in hearings, there's always someone in the room whose mission is stealing an image stamped with a smile—as if smuggling a prisoner out. These requests and attempts come from the knowledge that the images will proliferate on social media platforms to be viewed and interacted with. There is an organic understanding of how economies of images function, and how these images, in turn, circulate as signals. The smiling image says, "We have not yet been defeated," and it instructs a form of collective resilience that is unchallenged by the Israeli genocidal machine.[26] The image communicates its subject's desire for others to get up and perform a similar act, and therefore, its fabrication must be according to collectively practiced standards. The image is a call that awaits a response, it releases a sound in search of its echo. This genre of images isn't compelled by witnesses, it is looking for listeners.[27]

The mere act of smiling also complicates ethical questions surrounding the circulation of images of violence. The smile redirects the gaze from the broken limb, bloodied eye, and bruised torso towards kind faces that insist the struggle neither begins nor ends within the frames of images posturing as evidence. The colonial abuse becomes displaced and the image is repurposed to serve a political struggle rather than being left as colonial debris. By focusing on the smile over other details of the event of colonial confrontation, this form of image-making subverts habitual documentary visualities that oftentimes overexpose moments of spectacular violence inflicted on Palestinian bodies for the sake of mobilizing for a cause. Despite the urgency through which we consume and disseminate this genre of images, it is necessary to articulate the violence these images reproduce, particularly once plugged into economies of virtual circulation. Too often, virtual spaces are flooded with images of death and maiming that Zionism ostentatiously imposes on Palestinian life. And it is often Palestinians themselves, and their allies, who seek to document the occupation and expose its grotesque wrath, which can be a productive operation within specific registers. However, the hegemonic visualization that such documentary practices have produced reifies the inflicted repression, oftentimes leading to the fetishization of the wounded and abused Palestinian body. Such imagery also contributes, whether intentionally or passively, to power's demands to perpetually prove that power is violent and that its violence is efficient and profitable.[28] To put it differently, by making and disseminating imagery of spectacular violence, we succumb to the sovereign power's visual regime and its economic

25
See: Santiago Montag, "'Our Very Existence Here Is Our Resistance': Why Some Palestinians Smile When They Are Arrested by Israeli Soldiers." *Left Voice*, April 8, 2022. https://bit.ly/3AWtBWd.
; Mahmoud Soliman, "Smiling as an Act of Resistance in Occupied Palestine." *ROAR Magazine*, August 11, 2021. https://bit.ly/4dVxHMT.

26
Alaa Abd el-Fattah, *You Have Not Yet Been Defeated: Selected Works 2011-2021*. (United States: Seven Stories Press, 2022).

27
See: Fred Moten, "Black Mo'nin' in the Sound of the Photograph," in *In the Break: The Aesthetics of the Black Radical Tradition* (Minneapolis: University of Minnesota Press, 2003), 192-211.; Tina Campt, *Listening to Images* (Durham: Duke University Press, 2017), 3-45.

28
Palestine Action. "Dismantling Israel's War Machine." Edited by Joud Al-Tamimi. *Weird Economies*, April 24, 2024. https://weirdeconomies.com/contributions/dismantling-israel-s-war-machine.

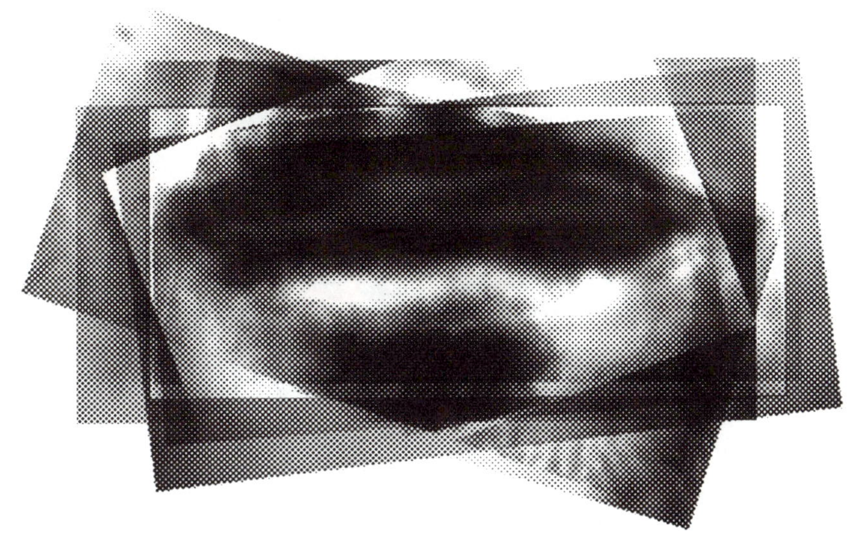

schemes that render cruel images into advertisements for the efficiency of the arms industry. We overexpose and hypervisibilize Palestinian bodies that have been subordinated under military colonial powers for decades in an attempt to situate an individual case as a representation of this system of subordination and colonization. When smiling is asked of violated bodies before an image freezes the moment of colonial abuse in a frame—excluding all time and space which exceed its framing, Palestinians bypass reproducing the violent image and instead produce a signal of steadfastness without compromising or obscuring the conditions within which this steadfastness is operating. We all know that the smiling subject has been and will be violated, but that doesn't mean this violation must be objectified, commodified, commercialized, or let alone overrepresented to the point of diminishing the fact that Palestinians aren't just victims, but persistent fighters who seek emancipation.

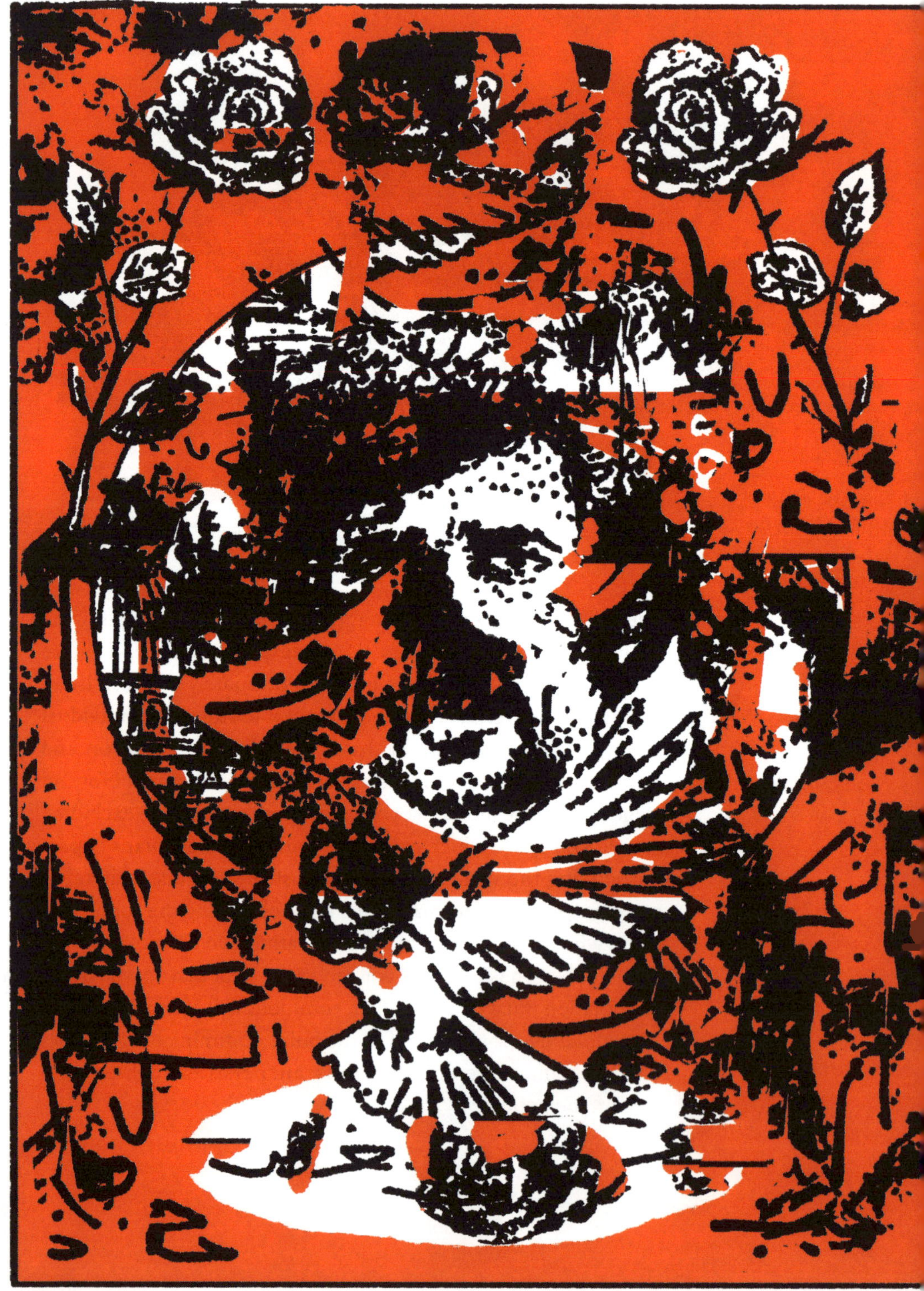

Mother,

I

have

وينك يما

disappeared

My image has left my home and gone to the streets. It could no longer bear the confinement, it needed to be outside. I walk and see my face plastered on the walls. It is a weird image of me that they have chosen. I see myself but I am no longer that person. The image stares back at me, alienating me, like a child seeing their reflection in the mirror for the first time, but it does not move as I move. It stays still. Sometimes, I feel so overwhelmed by my presence on the main road, my face plastered on street lights and concrete walls, on electricity boxes stationed outside of abandoned homes, sometimes multiplied in rows as if trying to conceal something behind them. When I wander off to the less frequented parts of town, I occasionally find pieces of me in funny corners. Yesterday, for instance, I saw my nose on the pavement. It felt as if someone had punched my nose off, but I felt nothing. The other day I saw my eyes, and I knew they were my eyes because they resembled my mother's. This is what my father always said, "you have your mother's eyes." I like it when I see pieces of me, fragments, little cuts. They are closer to me than the state of my face enlarged on a billboard.

At night, they say it's cold out. I often just sit on the stairs right by the square. I recall seeing someone ripping me off of a big wall and using me as a blanket. The tape that connected the posters of my faces to the wall made them look like a tapestry. I appeared in little digits. It seemed like it worked, keeping him warm. I used to be on the streets a lot, but the streets have become strange to me. I never thought this square where I spend my nights could be this quiet, this peaceful. They say that once your image reaches the streets it replaces you. You become your image, and then you're banned from joining the streets. Well, here I am, but I do feel displaced. My friend Faisal says it could be because of the rain.[29] *It's been washing me off the walls and into the sewage. It could also be because my face is spread out across town, or maybe it's the fragmentation of my face that is making me feel this way. It could be because, in some parts of town, new images are beginning to appear and cover those of mine. The new faces sometimes feel familiar, but I don't recognize them most of the time. I'm not sure how I feel about this, it's somewhat of a relief to not have my face everywhere. To be frank, sometimes I feel like there's so much of me to the point that I am no longer seen. I am everywhere and therefore I am nowhere. It could be a good thing that others are starting to take their turn. Is that selfish? I don't wish this on anyone, but it's difficult to walk in town when the only face you see is yours. When I see the faces of others appearing I feel comforted. It assures me that this is temporary. It's nice to be amongst others who share your experience. When my face disappears in the masses, it grants me anonymity. I like that. We keep each other company and hide in each other's shadows. It's only a small price to pay before we all disappear together, eventually.*

29
Faisal Darraj, *The Pitiable State of Culture in the Palestinian Establishment (būsu ạltẖāqāfati fī almūasasati alfilastīniati.)* (Beirut, Lebanon: Dar Al-Adab, 1996). (Arabic) 7-10.

2

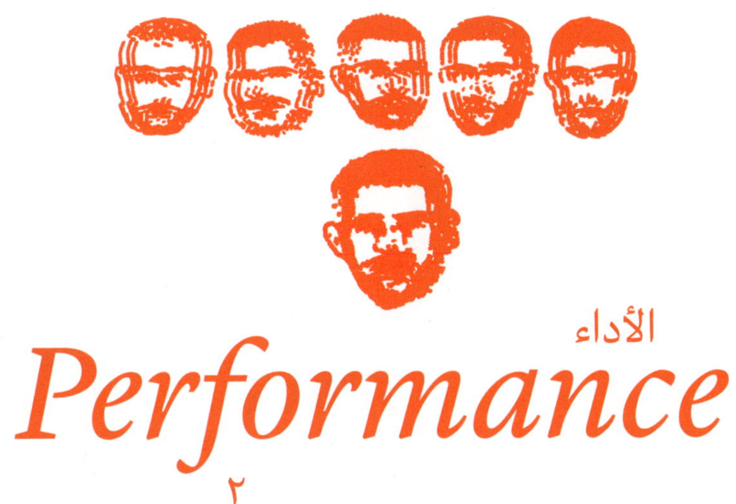

الأداء
Performance
٢

Dancing with our heads

على راسي وعيني

On October 8th, 2022, while Israeli troops were patrolling Shu'afat refugee camp in Jerusalem, Odai Tamimi, one of the camp's young men, went out to create an event of colonial confrontation in response to accelerating settlement projects in Jerusalem. Stealthily driving a rented car by the Israeli checkpoint which surveils anything and anyone that goes in and out of Shu'afat, Tamimi pulled out a stolen gun and fired at soldiers from a close range, killing one and injuring two others. He then disappeared into the night while Israeli authorities put out a call looking for him, describing him as a "bald Arab man dressed in a tracksuit." The Israeli occupation forces placed the camp under a blockade to find the young bald man they were looking for, conducting their habitual settler searches in homes, and stopping anyone whose profile matched Tamimi's.

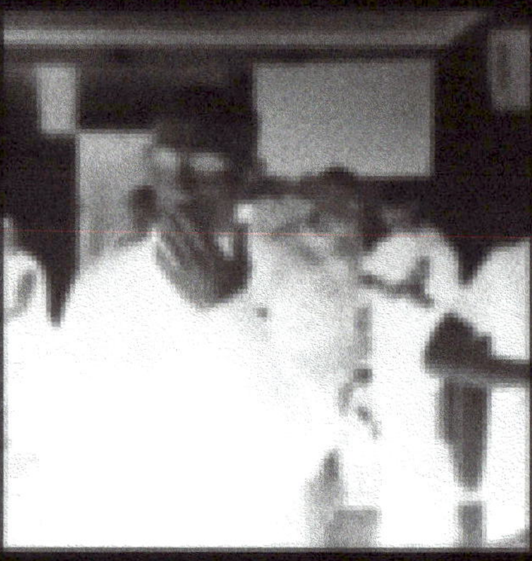

In a labyrinthine act of protection, Shu'afat's young male refugees decided to hijack the military's attempts to find Tamimi. Coopting the same colonial descriptives and racial profiling tropes utilized by Israeli surveillance technology to search for Tamini, the camp's residents created a mirage. The internet slowly began to flood with videos and images of Shu'afati men who had shaved their heads in homes and local barbershops, dressed in Adidas tracksuits in a manner that resembled Tamimi. They then dispersed as his clones throughout the refugee camp and the streets of Jerusalem, making the task of finding him impossible.[30] A congregation of Palestinians performed, for the colonial surveillance machine, exactly what it had scrutinized without allowing it to access *what it sought*. The bald heads in Jerusalem's streets built a protective shield, not with arms but with their bodies, to ensure Tamimi's safety by mimicking his colonially perceived guise. "With our heads, we safeguard the

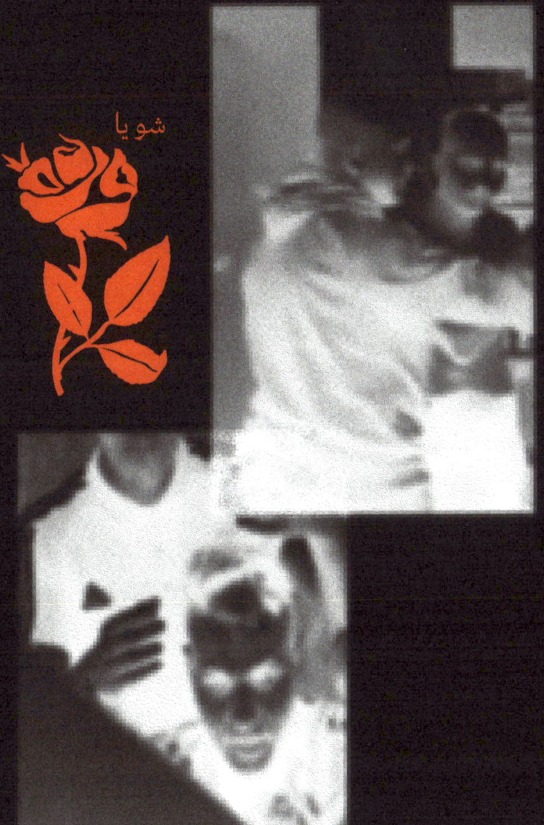

30
"Palestinian Youth Shave Their Heads to Confuse the Occupation Forces in Their Search for the the Executor of the Shu'afat Operation." Al Jazeera, October 15, 2022.https://bit.ly/3XnirS3.(Arabic).

31
The nomadic Palestinian tribes of *'arab al-sawahreh and badou al-jahhaleen* (بدو الجهالين و عرب السواحرة) were dispossessed of their lands in the naqab during the Nakba of 1948, then again during the Naksa of 1967 and resettled in Khan al-Ahmar. After the Oslo Accords, particularly in 1995-97, they were forcibly removed from Khan al-Ahmar for the third time, transferred through containers to the West Bank, and finally dispersed in areas surrounding Nablus, Jericho and Hebron. As activist Eid Abu-Ghaliah said, "The Bedouin Nakba is doubled, the first is to be forcibly removed from the lands in which you wonder, and the other is to be forced into settling in one place without movement, the severing from a nomadic way of being."

resistance" was the slogan they used for their maneuver, initiating a new form of resistance themselves, while executing a stratagem where street cameras were taken down and broken, and alleyways were blocked with burning tires—performing a militant dialectics of visibility and opacity.

A small disempowered and dismembered camp managed to delay the capture of Tamimi for two weeks through performance. On the night of October 20th, 2022, Odai Tamimi willingly revealed himself, carrying his body to its predictable demise by confronting Zionist soldiers with a gun, on his own, without protection or an intention to escape. He managed to infiltrate the settlement of Ma'ale Adumim, built on the ruins of Khan al-Ahmar, and opened fire at soldiers guarding the settlement.[31] He was shot multiple times while colonial steel punctured his body, causing him to collapse to the ground. Calculating his last breaths, he continued firing in the direction of the soldiers until his own fire became doused with blood. Tamimi was one of many who made individual sacrifices to challenge Israeli attempts at the liquidation of Palestinian resistance to its colonial project. But not every death is a death carried by many. Many fighters die in isolation, sometimes in solitary confinement after years of incarceration, others under the ruins of rubble that persists longer than a decomposing body. The Zionist death machine algorithmically measures the distance between us, the psychic capacities that define our drive, and the wounded social bonds at the brink of ripping apart, to compute a choreography of an isolating colonization, fragmenting us, destroying us. "With our heads, we safeguard the resistance" is a refusal to surrender to such a deathly choreography, a mortal dance. Instead, the young men of Shu'afat generated an embodied language of resistance and camaraderie from the negative.[32] Through aesthetics, militant assemblages are formed, languages and unquantifiable knowledge fabulated, and social amalgamations emerge despite all attempts of being eroded.

With these maneuvers, the supposedly fixed settler-colonial paradigm fails, and the roles are flipped. The power relation between the surveilling cameras and eyes of the occupiers, and the scrutinized bodies of Palestinians, is continuously challenged and refused. The young men of Shu'afat cease to exist as objects of observation, and become active performers who are consciously instrumentalizing their own monitored bodies. At the same time, the occupiers are repositioned as an audience, seated at the edge of their watchtowers with the imminent risk of falling. Their eyes plucked, their screens a stage. The young men of Shu'afat did not exit the colonial visual regime but carved out a negative space within it. They have used the most precarious aesthetic vessels available to them—their bodies—to create tensions, breaks, and fissures between presupposed conceptions of visibility, hypervisibility, opacity, and mimicry.

Revisiting these incidents is invigorating, it propels feelings of awe and even astonishment at the inventiveness of a collective spirit that refuses to be broken under such repressive conditions. But what compels many of us to consistently engage in a revolutionary aesthetic practice so parlous in its essence, due to the destituteness of its form, and the lethal outcome of its practicing, is the fact that we have nothing to lose, and the debt we accumulate (that which we owe and which is owed to us) will never be paid unless we abolish it ourselves.[33] These aesthetic forms of political resistance are a necessity for survival under a crushing settler-colonial entity that consistently labors towards the elimination of Palestinian presence on the land, and the total breaking of the Palestinian spirit so that resistance is deducted, eradicated, and liquidated from the equation. Three months after Odai Tamimi's martyrdom, on January 25th, 2023, over 300 Israeli troops invaded the Shu'afat refugee camp in an operation to demolish Odai Tamimi's family home.[34] The boys and men of the camp attempted to form a barricade with their bodies surrounding the late fighter's home, but the retaliation was brutal. Many Palestinians were subject to excessive beating and maiming, marking their bodies with bullet wounds and baton bruises, while others threw rocks at the soldiers from afar. Mohammad Ali Mohammad Ali, a 17-year-old native of the camp was shot, and even though he was rushed to the hospital, his body couldn't overcome the wounds it suffered. At dusk, he was pronounced dead, and Tamimi's home was declared a ruin.[35]

32
Basel Abbas and Ruanne Abou-Rahme, *May amnesia never kiss us on the mouth*, 2021–, https://mayamnesia.com

33
Denise Ferreira Da Silva, *Unpayable Debt*. (Germany: MIT Press, 2022). I have also written about this elsewhere in: Adam HajYahia. "The Principle of Return." *Parapraxis*, April 7, 2024.

34
All details about Tamimi's death, alongside descriptions of his demeanor and proceedings of demolishing his home can be found in the Zionist newspapers of Israel Hayom, Ynet and others, which I refuse to cite here due to their racist, colonial, and dehumanizing rhetoric.

35
Ibid.

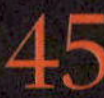

I am a specter, I am the Other

These embodied performative gestures are reminiscent of strategies that Palestinian women deployed during the Great Arab Revolt of 1936-39. At the time, workers went on strike, withholding their labor from British colonial authorities across the country. Farmers took up arms and instead of laboring their lands they became fighters in union with the land, protecting it from settlements, and the land in turn protected them. A lethal class of revolutionaries emerged to oppose and uproot British colonial governance over Palestine and its concomitant facilitation of accelerated Zionist settlement. Although colonial narratives of the event tried to frame it as sporadic criminal riots, it remains amongst the most costly organized anti-colonial upheavals that took place during the 20th century.[36] What is striking about that historical event, for our purposes, are the performative, sonic, and visual militant tactics used to counter colonial administration. These had to do with both gendered social dynamics prevalent within Palestinian society and the ways in which these dynamics were perceived and accordingly shaped by the Mandate government and its Zionist allies.

(ن)

(ف)

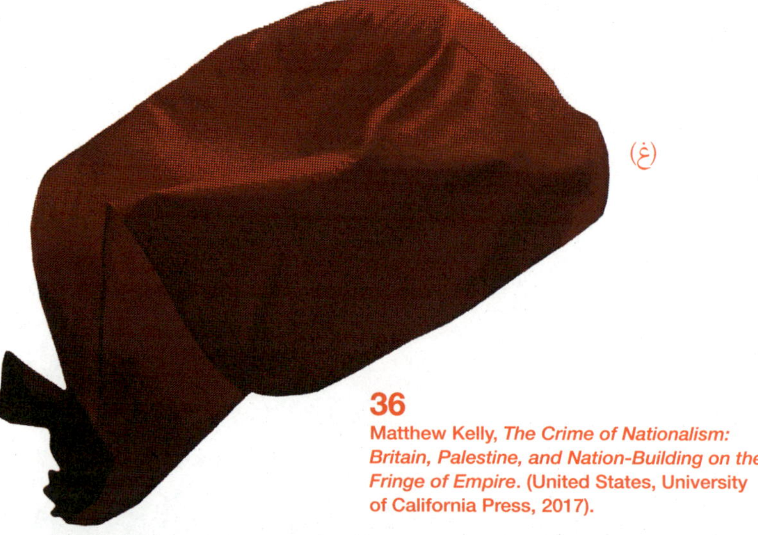
(غ)

36
Matthew Kelly, *The Crime of Nationalism: Britain, Palestine, and Nation-Building on the Fringe of Empire*. (United States, University of California Press, 2017).

During the years leading to the revolt, each social and political class, depending on their geography and dwellings, had the attire that signified their position/standing. Urbanite modern men wore tailored suits, while urbanite women dressed in buttoned shirts and skirts. Arab nationalists who lived in city centers wore a fez, or tarboosh, while businessmen who preferred to work with the English would forgo the hat. Farmer men and women wore long lightweight dresses to protect them from sun exposure while working the land for prolonged hours, and to keep them breezy. The men often wore the *hatta* and *agal* – the traditional headdress of various communities in the region made from a light cloth to cover the head (hatta), fixed with a doubled rope made of goat hair to keep the cloth attached (agal). Whereas the women wore the *tarha*, a light fabric that covers the head and shoulders, fixed to the head by shrouding the hair. All these signifiers materialized in varying attire carried with them social and political meanings both within Palestinian society and in the way they were perceived by the Mandate government and its personnel. And while they remained markers of class difference and political association, these signifiers were weaponized to communicate alternate meanings during the 1936 Revolt.

One particular request from the Palestinian nationalists during the years of the revolt is oftentimes brought up to criticize the Palestinian national struggle for its chauvinism. This request addressed women, as they were encouraged to begin wearing headscarves, across social, political, urban, and peripheral class lines. Although the patriarchal social order in Palestine undoubtedly remains pervasive, this particular historical request bore additional motives. This is not to dismiss patriarchal social organization, nor to hierarchize conditions of violence, or prioritize certain subjects of violence over others, only to then make assessments on which structures require more urgency. But to forge an analysis of political and depoliticized subjectivities, and the ways these subjectivities resist, despite their implication

(س)

(ح)

in interlocking structures of repression. The logic underpinning the expectation to wear the headscarves demanded of women was formulated as a militant strategy to bewilder the colonizing enemy, while nonetheless maintaining patriarchal-nationalist restructurings of Palestinian society, and Palestinian women understood this paradigm and navigated it towards their subjective political ends.

As a response to the British colonization and Zionist settlement, Palestinians challenged the identity of the "nation" and scored it with signifiers that allude to a collective sense of unity against attempts of erasure and claims of nonexistence. Palestine of the revolt witnessed the modern resurgence of classical Arab attire, as many returned to practicing traditions reserved for the classes of farmers and rural communities. The hatta and agal made a comeback for men across social, urban, and political strata of society, and as such, an equivalent headdress–the headscarf–was demanded of women to complete this national aesthetic unification process. In this way, the revolutionary subject of the revolt embodied in the figures of the farmer or the worker whose visual performative signifiers were their clothes, became nationalized and reproduced into those not presumed to be engaged in revolutionary action. Performing for the colonial gaze, the urbanite 'weak' man and the 'non-revolutionary' city and village woman who wanted to belong to the nation in its fight against the empire dressed similarly to those who were conceived as the fighters. In other words, the lines were blurred between so-called politicized revolutionary subjects (farmer men) and socialized domesticized subjects (women and urban men).

This unification had militant valence beyond its symbolic value. Preceding the revolt, the British-Zionist alliance consistently monitored Palestinians crossing wildlands from their watchtowers and military outposts, distinguishing their social position from their silhouettes and attire. Meaning, the headdress would automatically differentiate farmers from non-farmers, and the suit would identify the businessmen from the militants and men from women. After the return to classical customs, it became harder for Britons and their cronies to distinguish between those crossing the lands to transfer arms, those traveling to buy or sell crops, and the aimless wanderers. What became interesting as these performativities unfolded, was not how men instrumentalized women for their anti-colonial projects, but how women instrumentalized the social-colonial order within which they have been produced as domestic subjects, to embed themselves within the struggle for political autonomy and the liberation of themselves and their land.

Oral histories and collective memory testify how many women seemingly performed a colonial sexual projection of their colonized domesticity, while in reality, they were completely embedded in the struggle for the liberation of Palestine without needing to bear arms or perform a limited imagination of what constitutes anticolonial militancy.[37] This political dimension which is performed through the social realm is illustrated vividly in Heiny Srour's 1984 film *Leila and the Wolves*, where Palestinian women, throughout historical events, are seen as actively engaged in the militant struggle for liberation. Their engagement, as seen through Srour's eyes, is not visualized through their hypervisible carrying of Kalashnikovs or other arms but through their seemingly banal performance of domestic labor: carrying large amounts of food and crops from one place to another; singing and dancing in social events such as wedding festivities, and enacting other traditional ceremonies relegated to the social and banned from the political. However, the film reveals these activities to us as inherently political, because hidden within the baskets of wheat women carried on their heads were arms and ammunition. Underneath the festive sounds of singing and dancing, collective councils were held to plan the next attack on the colonizing enemies. And the adornment of golden bridal jewelry turned out to be repurposed as a form of transferring resources from one locality to another. This complication of social roles and dimensions is afforded to us once we recognize the performances of women concerning their feminized domesticity via their aesthetic fluency in deploying such strategies politically. Palestinian women weren't only conscious of the patriarchal conditions that determined their socialized roles but also of their perception as colonized women by the colonizing enemy. They performed their colonized domesticity to Zionist and British colonists while they also hijacked the patriarchal social order within which they lived amongst men at large.

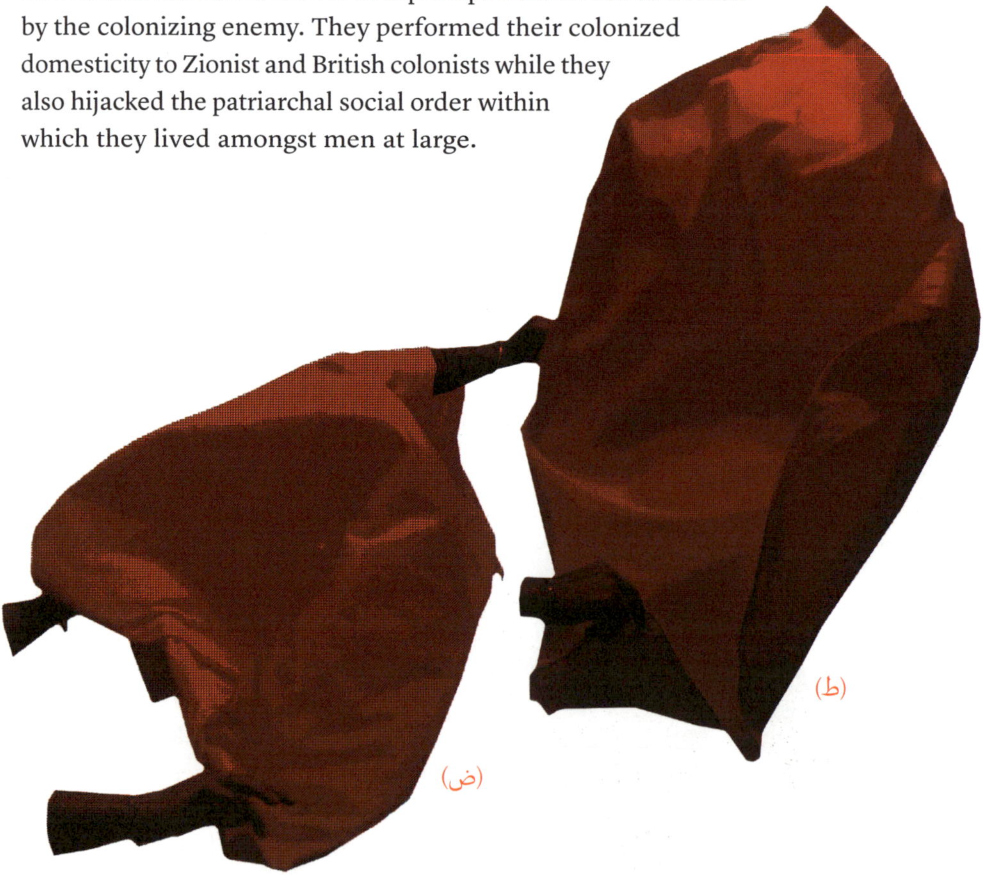

(ط)

(ض)

37
It is interesting to think through Luce Irigaray's critique of Freud where feminine subjectivity—only seen through the way it has been theorized as a subjugated subjectivity formulated through negation to man—is performed by women who understand this paradigm. Woman only performs the limited phallogocentric view of herself, which is what is legible to the European male. If to him anything outside of that view will be pathologized, why would she trouble herself with proving him wrong? See: Irigaray, Luce. *Speculum of the other woman.* Ithaca, N.Y: Cornell Univ. Press, 2010. 46-61.

A Choreography of

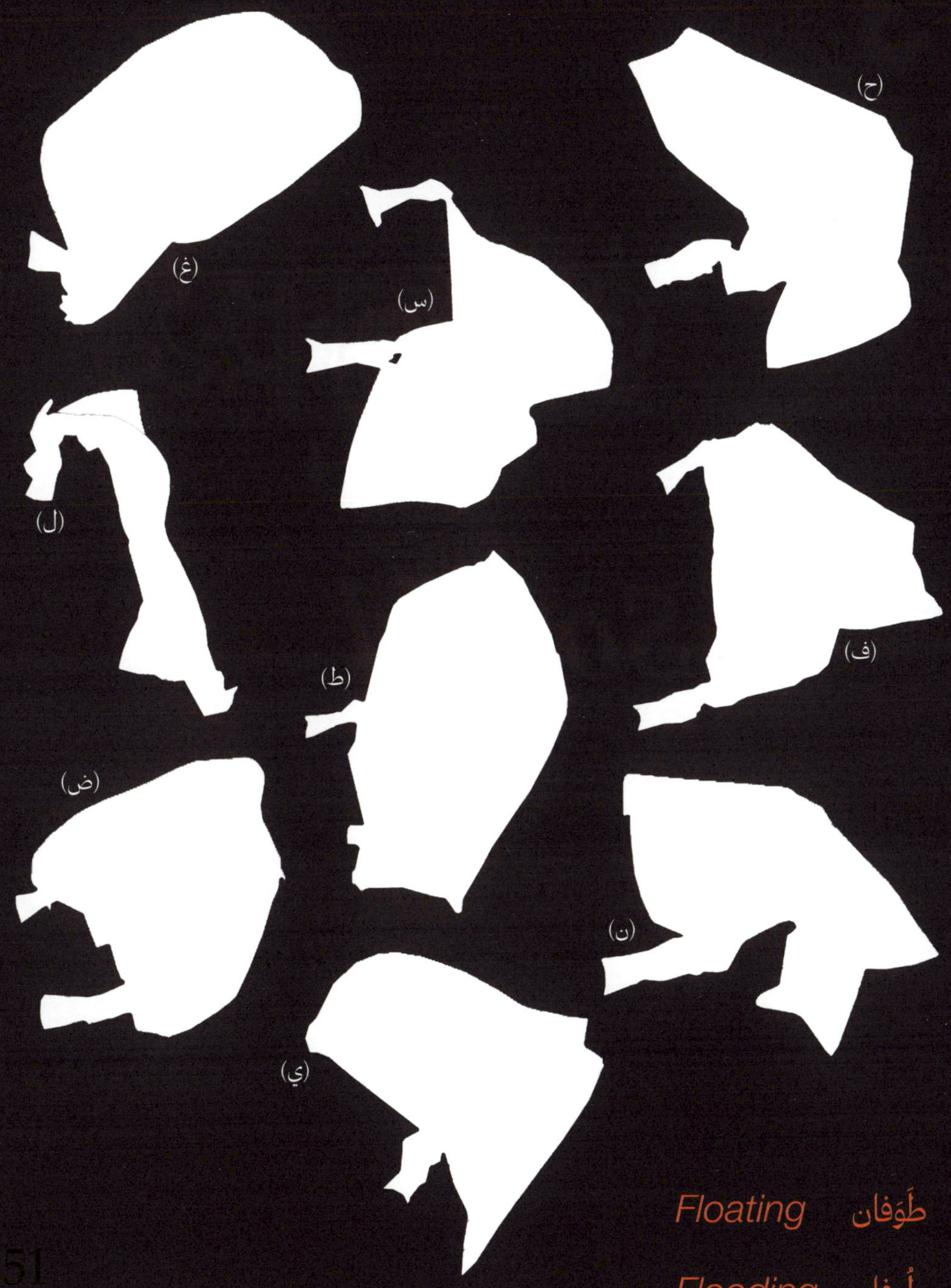

Floating طَوفان

Flooding طُوفان

3

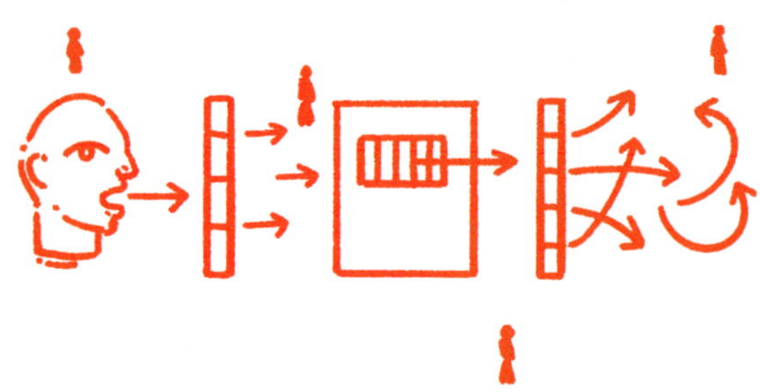

صوت
Sound
٣

The echoes of such aesthetic strategies developed during the years of the revolt, performative, sonic, and otherwise, reverberate to this very day. Writing about the 1936 Great Arab Revolt (*al-thawra al-kubra*), or as the Zionist colonial intelligence unit the Haganah called them: the "events"—which simultaneously opposed the British Mandate, capitalist exploitation of landless farmers, the heightening of racialized class relations, and Zionist settlement in Palestine—Matthew Kelly examines the criminalizing framework of the British Mandate as a counter-revolutionary tool of depoliticization.[38] The domain which he calls the "crimino-political" in the case of the Mandate, which operated on both discursive and legal grounds, used the category of the criminal synonymously with that of an Arab nationalist, formalizing anti-colonial and anti-capitalist political organizing as a crime. It is not a coincidence that The 1936 Code Ordinance was completed and put into effect in September of that year, five months after the eruption of the revolt, as it was used as the solid foundation through which colonial jurisprudence attempted to topple what had threatened its validity.[39] This is how the 1936-39 Great Arab Revolt produced the largest number of incarcerated Palestinians under the Mandate government, but what it had also produced was an emergent aesthetic tradition of revolt—the fabulation of a novel form for political organization.

Unlike images, which are easily commodifiable, captured in frame, enclosed, frozen in time, marked with value, and dispossessed as they circulate, sound and music are immaterial, fleeting, piercing, and moving. Sound travels, it seeps, slips, and bleeds. If loud enough it damages, if low, muffled, deadened, or mute it unsettles, and at other times escapes. Colloquially known as *mshaffarat* in Arabic —meaning "coded" in the feminine plural, Palestinian women developed a genre of songs encrypted with lyrical, melodic, and compositional structures that conceal political messages delivered

38
Matthew Kelly, *The Crime of Nationalism.*

39
Matthew Hughes "The banality of brutality: British Armed forces and the repression of the Arab revolt in Palestine, 1936-39'." *The English Historical Review*,124 (507) (2009): 313 - 354.

to prisoners. The logic of mshaffarat is that they emerge out of existing Palestinian folkloric singing traditions, which oftentimes evoke the immediate lived reality of Palestine. From rain-summoning songs in seasons of drought, to songs to and of the land that sustains life, to songs about farmers and merchants who travel afar with prayers for their safe return, and others about the hardships and challenges of land grab, dispossession, and the struggle for sovereignty. Mshaffarat, however, aren't simply songs. It is through their misleading form as folkloric and trivial that they proliferated unguarded, while indexed within their deceptively disarming form are political messages in search of those equipped with listening. This is why mshaffarat are both ubiquitous and exceptional. In a sense, they resemble other songs and evoke other melodies. They are likely to be sung in various contexts, such as during harvest seasons or weddings. When Palestinian women would go visit British and Zionist prisons with their loved ones and comrades held captive, it wasn't be an oddity for them to sing on the outside as they waited, or during visitation. They would sing their songs there as they did elsewhere.

The most referenced song from this genre in contemporary times, which is popular and known to many Palestinians due to its proliferation as a folksong amongst many commercial musicians, is *Ya Taali'een el-Jabal* (O' You, Going Up the Mountain). The roots of this song are anchored in the hot soils of the 1936 revolt; as fighters turned into captives, the women of the revolt marched towards the prisons to sing for them.

The song belongs to a specific lineage of mshaffarat, which all use the same encoding logic, known as *molalaah*. Ya Taali'een el-Jabal, like other molalaahs, was coded using two technical systems. The first is in the way it is sung: the song's lyrics unfold unintelligibly for unfamiliar ears due to the addition of extra syllables with the letter L followed by a vowel in between letters and words, eclipsing the words with a recurring sound. With tongue trills and repetitive fillers, the pronounced words are obscured. The opening lyrics in practice are, *Ya Taali' een een ellelel-Jabal Ya Molelelmol Elmoqideen elNar* concealing *Ya Taali'een el-Jabal Ya elMoqideen elNar,* meaning, *O' you, going up the mountain, setting fire ablaze.* The second is through poetic meaning: once the actual lyrics concealed behind the sounds are revealed, they must undergo a second round of interpretation for meaning to be extracted. Unlike other class societies, reading, writing, and poetry weren't reserved for those benefiting from the exploitation of laborers. Fluency in poetics and linguistic complexity were and remain a *common* shared by the vast majority of society. Uninterrupted by ululations, the lyrics read:

O' you, going up the mountain,
setting fire ablaze
Safety is what I wish for you,
O' beloved ones
I do not wish for gowns,
nor do I wish for girdles
Safety is what I wish for you,
O' beloved ones
To those gazelles inside,
entrapped inside
Safety is what I wish for you,
O' beloved ones
To those gazelles inside,
this will no longer last
Safety is what I wish for you,
O' beloved ones[40]

40

يا طالعين عين الجبل
يا مول الموقدين النار
بين يامان يامان عين الهنا يا روح
ما بدي منكي لكم خلعة
ولا بدي ملبوس
بين يامان يامان
عين الهنا يا روح
ما بدي منكي لكم خلعة ولا بدي زنار
بين يامان يامان
عين الهنا يا روح
إلا غزال الذي جوين لكم محبوس
بين يامان يامان
عين الهنا يا روح
إلا غزال الذي جوّين لكم ما يدوم
بين يامان يامان
عين الهنا يا روح

Sung as a farewell for those embarking on trips away from home, this song was addressed, in fact, to those forced to go nowhere: the imprisoned fighters of the Mandate government and its Zionist allies. *O'you, going up the mountain,* references the Palestinian fighters on the ground, preparing to come for a rescue mission of those who are jailed. The women would sing to inform *those gazelles inside,* the incarcerated fighters, to watch out and prepare themselves to be set free, for their entrapment *will no longer last.* The cue for this mission, what announces its beginning and declares its execution is the *setting* of *fire ablaze.* The women would alert *those gazelles inside* to watch out for the burning fire seen through the cracks in the walls and the windows of the prison to prepare for their escape right before the fighters arrive.

There are numerous other genres of coded songs, each with its own system of encryption and messaging. The ones that are no longer in political use are familiar and recorded enough to be referenced here, while others are in constant evolution through a persistent practice to this very day, unrecorded, and as such they shall remain. These mshaffarat were developed as a musical form at the plight of modernity in Palestine, in the transition from rule under the Ottoman Empire into colonization by the British and settlement by the Zionists. It was a militant aesthetic strategy born out of a necessity to resist colonial governance and the technologies it developed and tested on the colonized world, in spite of the lack of availability of military technologies or powerful armies. They emerged precisely from this lack, this indebtedness, this precarity, as an aesthetic form interlocked with a political project. Like a stone catapulting into the besieging walls of Mandate prisons, mshaffarat inscribed in sound circumvented the edifices of surveillance, governance, and colonial rule. Dismissed as women whose banning from the political and their confinement to the patriarchal-social deemed them unthreatening, and as racialized native women with cultural traditions adverse to the colonial canon, their singing bore no apparent peril to colonial governance. As their ululations infiltrated the highly secured prisons, they raised no alarm. Their delivering and deliverance through feminized bodies rendered them invisible. The sounds were deemed extraneous because the bodies that generated them were conceptualized as socially peripheral within patriarchal-colonial-racial dogmas. This peripherality of feminine and feminized Palestinian bodies and the negativity ascribed to them rendered the sound they have produced to appear ghostly. Uttered and performed right at the frontiers of colonial establishments of carcerality, they transgressed unseen.

The dialectic between the sonic and the visual, images that speak and sounds that are invisible, replete in Palestine's revolutionary tradition, emerged in tandem with the crystallization of the national anticolonial struggle, and from within the structure of the settler-colonial catastrophe. It propels a form of knowing that isn't instituted in regulated systems of recording, documentation, and archiving yet is one that is stored in the muscles of the repressed. Instinctually, these classes of knowledge emerge and re-emerge generation after the other as aesthetic traditions of revolt inscribed in the revolting vessels we embody, and transmitted through sensory social experience.

Social upheavals in the streets of Palestine show us how such an aesthetic language is rarely planned, and seldom initiated through processes of discussion and conspiration, yet ones embedded in an aesthetic language of embeddedness in struggle. It is a language of poverty. It is a language of precarity. A language borne through the reality of the negative as ongoing catastrophe. A language that activates the ruination and ruin, the site of extraction, the paraphernalia of settler-colonial disfigurement, the wounded and maimed body, and its images and representations. Language as excess and detritus. Whether it is a smile or a wink at a camera lens, a coded song infiltrating a prison cell, a piece of poetry on a slice of tissue smuggled out during visitation hours,[41] digging a hole out of prison with a spoon to announce the great escape,[42] playing music in bars and brothels to conceal political speech undergoing monitoring, or to fly high above in the air to overcome besieging walls that lock generations from reaching the sky, these are all accumulating in this negative that persists time and again. Tradition of the oppressed, aesthetics of the repressed.

41
See: Layan Kayed, "Prison As a Text," *Majallat Al-Dirasat al-Filastiniyya (Journal for Palestine Studies)* Prisoners' Words.. Springs of Speech, no. 128 (August 2021): 201–6; 1;. Kaleem Hawa, "Like a Bag Trying to Empty," *Parapraxis*, parapraxismagazine.com/articles/like-a-bag-trying-to-empty.

42
The Gilboa Prison Break on 6 September 2021, where Ayham Nayef Kamamj, Mahmoud Abdullah Ardah, Mohamed Qassem Ardah, Monadel Yaqoub Nafe'at, Yaqoub Mahmoud Qadri, and Zakaria Zubeidi dug up a tunnel, creating an escape route out of one of the most high-security Zionist prisons, with advanced surveillance carceral technology, only using a spoon.

1

An image/face/word/ flower resurfaced on my screen, then dissolve with a tap.

2

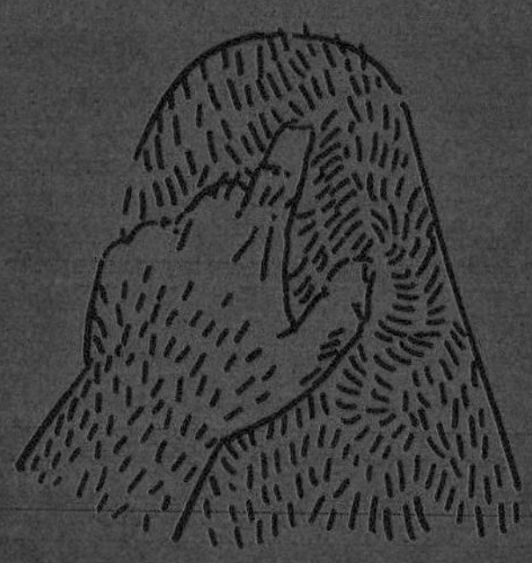

I keep tracing an image/ face/word/flower on my thigh with my finger.

3

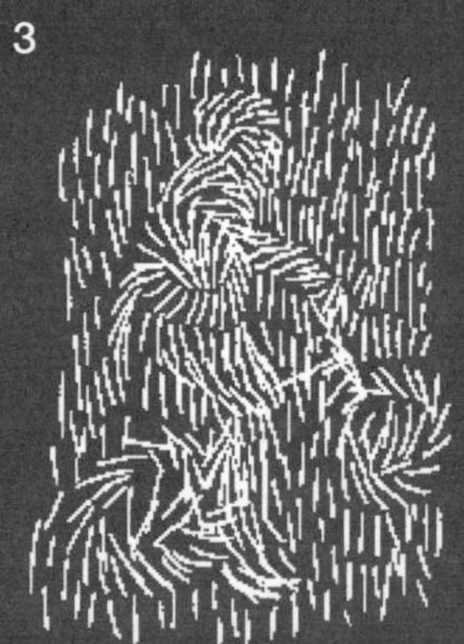

The markings turn into faded features from the grease on my fingertips and the hairs on my thigh.

4

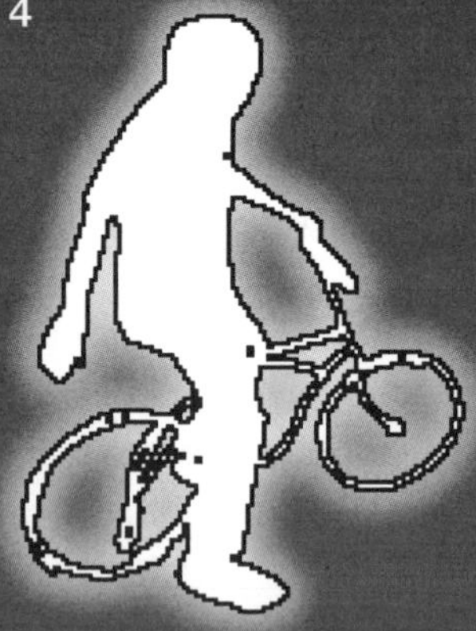

The features are now faded lines on paper.

5

The lines resurface as engravings on my skin, alongside other images/faces/words/flowers that once haunted me before.

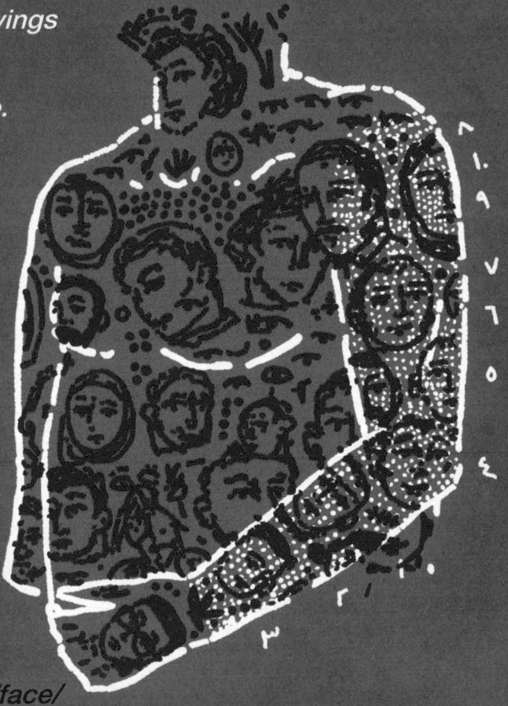

6

I wonder if giving this image/face/word/flower a longer lifetime

will it have more grace. . .

A longer time to linger in my mind,

and a longer time to fade away.

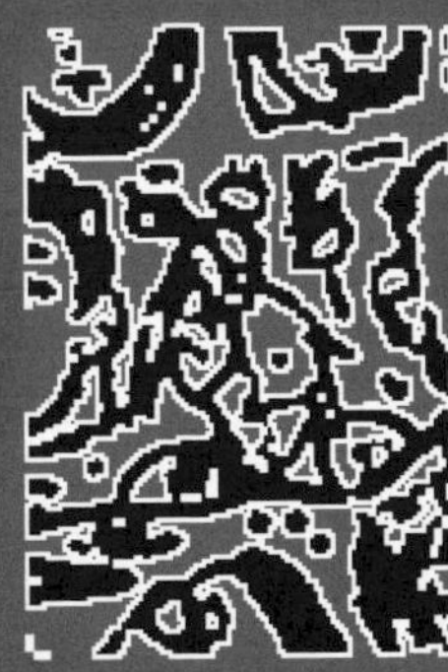

7

I took a photo of my skin with the image/face/word/flower.

Now it has returned to my screen.

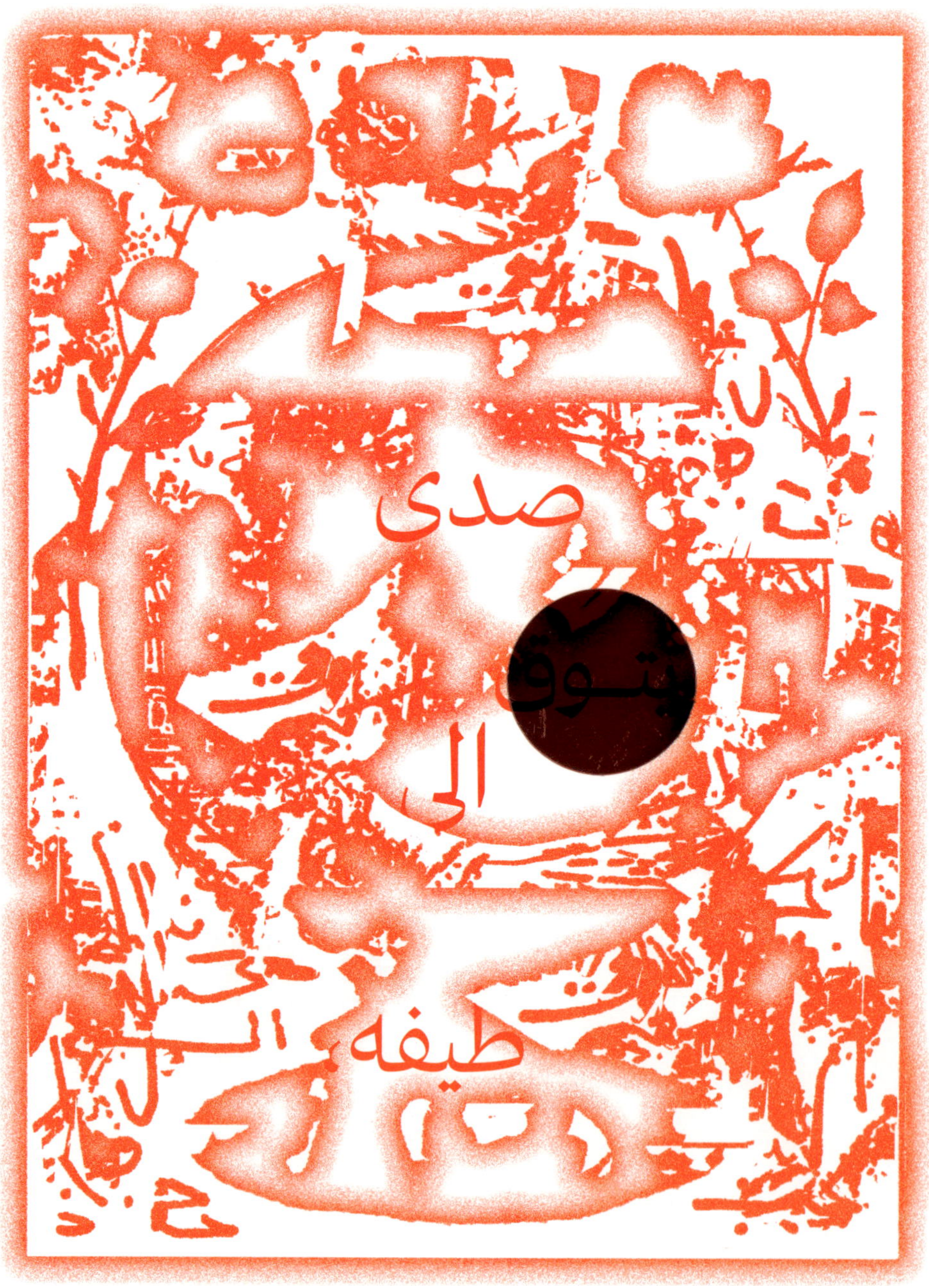

جماليّات المكبوت

آدم حاج يحيى
و
هيثم حدّاد

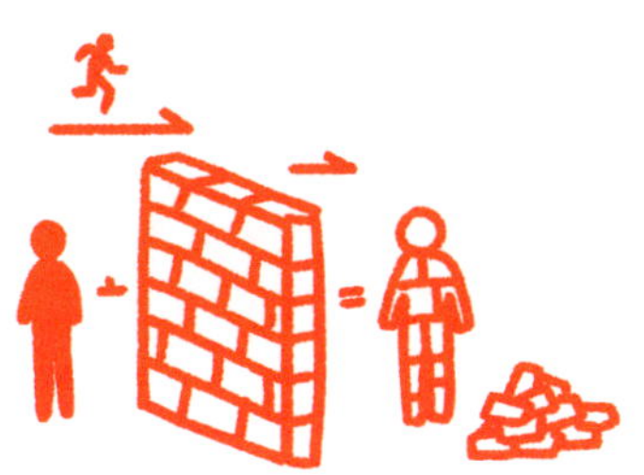

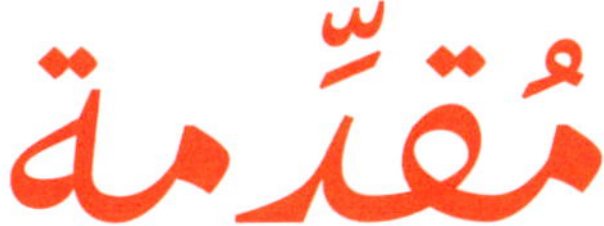

جمالك

جمال

مش عادي

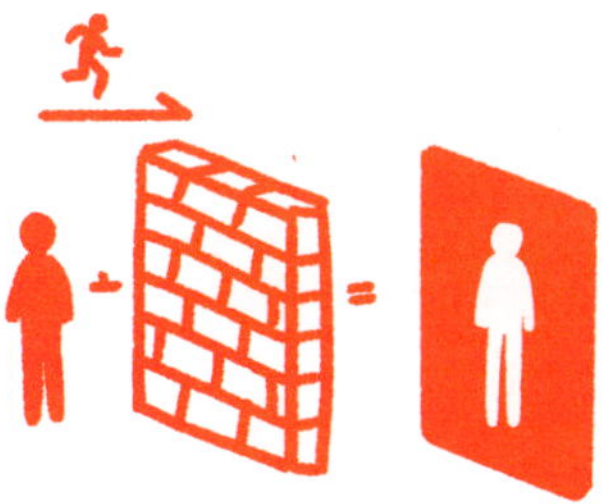

أو

جماليّات المكبوت

تُحْدِثُ الانتفاضات والثورات شيئًا يتجاوز أن يكون ضمنيًا فَحسب. كيف ولماذا يتيقَّظ الناس في آن واحد دون أي تخطيطٍ مُسبق؟ خاصَّة في مجتمع معاصر يتَّسم بالاغتراب والاستهلاك والفردانية. كيف ننهض و نصحو في الوقت نفسه وبذات الطريقة إذا كنا، قبل الحَدَث الذي طال انتظاره، نعيش حيوات مُلَبرَلة[1] منفصلة؟ في نهاية المطاف، وعلى الرغم من نضالاتنا المُجزَّأة، فلسنا جميعًا مُنغمسين في النضال، ولا مَنظّمين سياسيين نكرّس أنفسنا للسياسات الجماعية. إن افتراض الـ«نحن» بحد ذاته يُشكِّل حقل ألغام من الإشكاليات والتقديرات التي يتعيَّن علي«نا» التعامل معها، فيما تسقي الدماء أراضٍ دون أخرى. ومع ذلك، فإن هذه التمييزات والتفريقات والتسلسلات الهرمية لا تُقرِّبنا من تكوين الوحدة الاجتماعيّة. بل إن الاعتراف بالاختلاف باعتباره دلالة متأصلة على التعددية والجماعية غير المتجانسة (خارج أهداف إنتاج القيمة) هو الذي قد يقودنا إلى تشكيل مجتمع غير مُلَبرَل على الرغم من التشكيل النيوليبرالي للذوات. إنه الإصرار على إبقاء الاختلاف والتوترات والخِلافات والإحباطات كفضاء سلبي داخل الجسم الاجتماعي الذي يرفض التجانس والهيمنة حتى تستديم صحته. ومع ذلك، لا يزال ينهض الكثيرون منا جماعيًا في لحظات معينة وبأشكال معينة لخلق صدع سياسي، على الرغم من تقلقُل البنى التحتية التنظيمية السياسية وغياب جسم اجتماعي يحقق ذلك. إذًا، كيف نصحو جماعيًا؟ كيف نجد أنفسنا وسط حَدَث سياسي ككتلة موّحدة؟

١ مُلبرَل أي حوّله الى ليبرالي.

إن الإجـابة البسيـطة، أو بالأحـرى القصيـرة، هي أن حيواتنـا تتشـكّل وتتشبّع بالـعنف. وإن تصعيـد هذا الـعنف إلـى مستويـات قصوى ومظاهر مـروّعة هـو الذي يدفعنـا إلـى حـافّة الهـاوية، حيث مـا من إمـكانٍ سـوى المقـاومة والمواجـهة. يمـكن لتقاليـد المـاضي أن تُظهِـر لنـا كيف ولمـاذا نـنهض ونقـاوم، لكنهـا تشيـر أيضًـا إلـى كمـون العديـد من الاحتجاجـات والثـورات الاجتمـاعية السيـاسية التي ظـلّت مُعـلّقة في الزمن، علـى الرغـم من توفّـر الظـروف البنيـوية الـعنيفة التي من المفتـرض أن تـحفّز انـدلاع الانتفـاضة أو الثـورة. إن واقـع الشـعوب المضطهـدة تاريخيًـا وتلـك التي لا تزال تتحمّـل الـعنف الشـديد من دون أن تصـل قـط إلـى شـرارة التـعبئة الجمـاعية، وتجـربة الشـعوب الأخـرى التي قـاومت، وتلـك التي تواصـل المقـاومة في عزلة وانحبـاس، لا تزال تُشكّل لُغزًا بشأن مـا إذا كان يجب الجزم بالأُخـرويَّة الثـورية أو معارضتهـا.

لـكن بين لـحظة الاعتـراف بالـعنف الذي يظهـر علـى الجلـد وذاك المحجـوب تحتـه ولـحظة العمـل الجمـاعي، هنـاك عمـلية نفـسية مـادية تُيسّـر التحـول. هنـاك تركيبـات وجـدانيّة ومُجسّـدة ومعـرفيّة تعمـل علـى استفزاز مثـل هذه العمليـات أو تصعيدهـا أو دعمهـا. وإذا لـم تـكن أفعـال الـكلام هي التي تُحـرِّك الأنـسجة الاجتمـاعية، و تـحفّز الانتفاضـات والثـورات، فلا بـد أن يكـون هنـاك شيء آخـر، ربمـا حِسِّي الطابـع، يجمـع الجماهيـر. إنهـا ***الجماليات***.

صـاغ جـاك رانسييـر الجماليـات، في مشـروعه الفلسـفي المستمـر لتحديد القواعـد التي تُدعِّـم الـعلاقة المتبـادلة بين السيـاسة والجماليـات، باعتبارهـا النظـام الذي يحكـم «توزيـع المحسـوس» أو «نظـام الأشـكال المُـسبقة التي يُحـدِّد مـا يعـرض نفسـه للتجـربة الحـسية»[٢]. ووفقًـا لرانسييـر، إذا كانت السيـاسة تجريبية/تعتمـد علـى الخبـرة - كمـا هـو الحـال في استنادهـا إلـى الخبـرة الحـسية قبـل أن تُحـوَّل إلـى فكـر، وبالتـالي إلـى كلام أو فعـل - فأين هـو الشـكل الجمـالي، والجماليـات بشـكل عـام، كنظـام يحكـم توزيـع الخبـرة الحـسية نفسـها التي من

٢
Jacques Rancière, *The Politics of Aesthetics* (United Kingdom: Bloomsbury Publishing, 2013), 13-14.

خلالها تُولَد السياسة؟ في صياغته للشكل الجمالي من خلال وظيفته المحدَّدة، يكتب رانسيير قائلًا «إن [الجماليات تعني] ترسيم حدود الأمكنة والأزمنة، والمرئي وغير المرئي، والكلام والضوضاء، وهو الترسيم الذي يُحدِّد في الوقت نفسه مكان ومخاطر السياسة كشكل من أشكال الخبرة. تدور السياسة حول ما يُرى وما يمكن قوله عمَّا يُرى، وحول من لديه القدرة على الرؤية ومن يمتلك موهبة الكلام، وحول خصائص الأمكنة وإمكانيات الزمن».

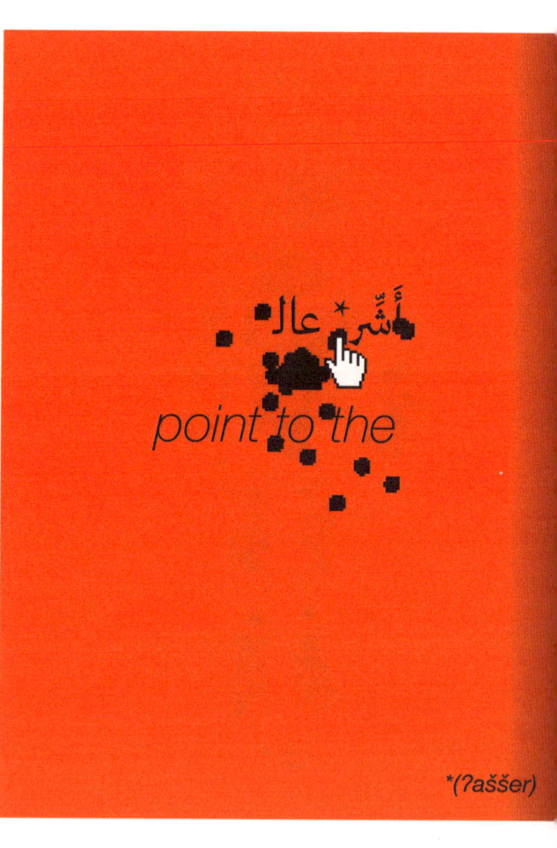

وعلى هذا النحو، فإن الجماليات ترفد التجربة السياسية: فالسياسة ليست الأنظمة الاجتماعية أو السياسية التي أنشأناها للتجمُّع والحُكم والتنظيم بشكل رسمي وغير رسمي. إنها التجارب الحِسية المنقوشة في الشكل الجمالي، ومن خلاله، قبل أن تتحول إلى فكر أو كلام أو فعل. وعلى هذا النحو، فإن القمع والتعبير والحرية والاستعباد ظروف مُقيَّدة بطبيعة التجربة الحسية ومدى القُدرة و**اللاقُدرة** على الإحساس[٣].

٣

إن المُداخلة النظرية لجاسبير بوار حول معنى اللاقُدرة مهمة هنا. تكتب بوار عن اللاقُدرة كفئة بايوسياسية تُستخدم جنبًا إلى جنب مع الإعاقة والاستطاعة، فتكشف في الوقت نفسه عن حدودهما المفاهيمية والتاريخية وتوضِّح اعتمادهما المتبادل. وتُحاجج بوار بأن اللاقُدرة تكوين جسدي يحدث من خلال العنف السياسي الرأسمالي والقمعي الذي يُحدِّد فعليًا شروط مشاركة واستبعاد جسد المرء في الاجتماعي والسياسي. تصبح اللاقُدرة بحد ذاتها مثيرة للاهتمام باعتبارها إصابة حرفية ومجازية للجسد تُشوِّه وتَحِد من تجربة المرء الحسية (قدرته الحسية في الواقع)، وبالتالي مشاركته في النظام الجمالي - اللاقُدرة باعتبارها إضفاء العجز على الإحساس، اللاقُدرة باعتبارها تمكينًا «لبعض أشكال الحياة وتثبيطًا لأشكال أخرى». انظر/ي

Jasbir K. Puar, *The Right to Maim: Debility, Capacity, Disability*. Durham: Duke University Press, 2017. Preface xiv-xxi.

تتجلى الأحداث السياسية عند رانسيير حصريًا داخل هذا النظام الجمالي، من خلال إنتاج أو تجميع لحظات صدع في النظام الحاكم. يعني هذا أن الأحداث السياسية لا تحدث جدليًا (ديالكتيكيًا) في نظام رانسيير للمحسوس، ولكن من خلال حدث تجميعي يكشف عن مفهوم «إنساني» فطري للمساواة يتحدّى المشاركة غير الموزّعة بالتساوي في النظام الجمالي. بعبارة أخرى، لا تترك جماليات رانسيير الديمقراطية أي مجال للسلبية، لأنها لا تتصوَّر قيمة سلبية داخل الشكل السياسي. بحسب رانسيير، في الحَدَث السياسي، ترتقي الجماعة المضطهَدة أو المجردة من إنسانيتها بحيث تُتصوَّر ويُعترَف بها على أنها مساوية للجماعة المضطهِدة من خلال تكوين جمالي ما. والتحول الذي يُصاغ في هذه اللحظة السياسية الخاصة ليس جدليًا، بمعنى أن المُضطهَد والمضطهِد - المُتولّى والمولَى - لا يتحولان من خلال علاقة تؤثّر عليهما معًا، بل من خلال اعتراف المضطهِد بمساواة من يضطهده. وهذا الاعتراف بالمساواة هو اعتراف بالقدرة الحسية المتساوية المشتركة بين المضطهِد والمضطهَد، والتي كانت حتى «لحظة الصدع» محكومة بشكل غير متساوٍ من قِبل طغيان النظام المهيمن. باختصار، على الرغم من القواسم المشتركة المفترضة في القدرة الحسية والمعرفة، هناك تسلسل هرمي للمشاركة في التجربة الحسية، والمَزْق في هذا التسلسل الهرمي هو الذي يُتصوَّر على أنه السياسة.

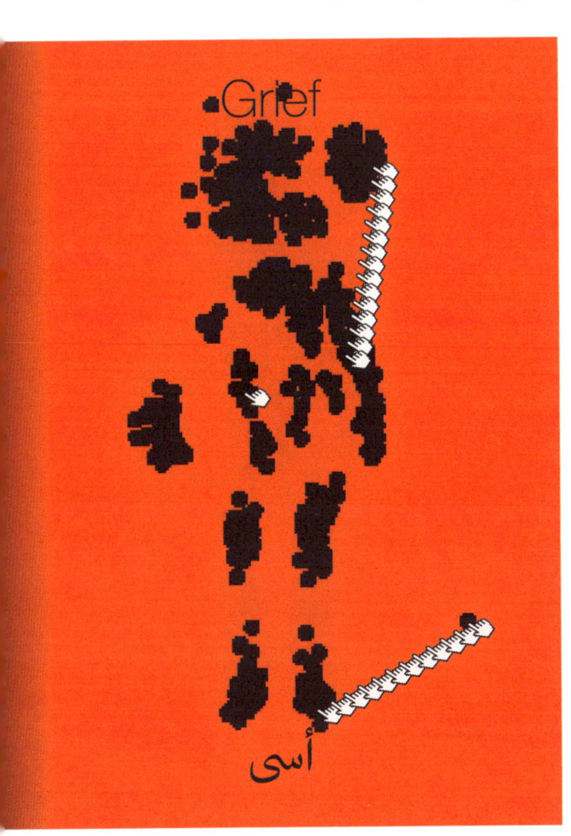

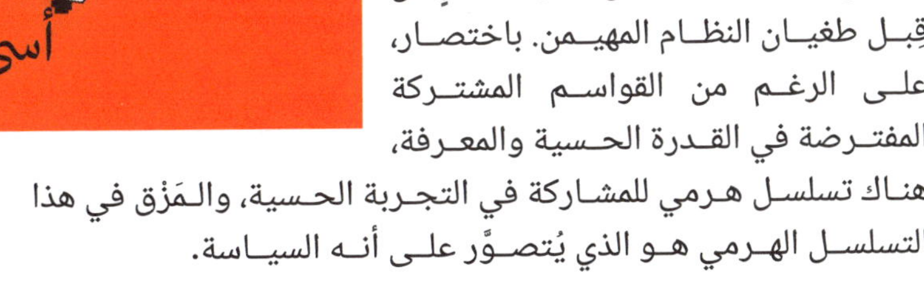

في السياقات السياسية العنيفة التي تُفرِط في إشباع تجاربنا وتواصل انتزاع مستقبلنا - الاستعمار والتشريد والإبادة والاستعباد والسجن - تَضعف المفاهيم المتعلقة بالمساواة وتفقد أي قيمة جذرية تزعم أنها تَعِد بها. توفِّر المفاهيم الديمقراطية للمساواة وإجراءاتها التصنيفية مساحةً محدودة للفعل السياسي في أفضل الأحوال، وفي

أسـوأ الأحـوال تُبطِـل السيـاسة بميولهـا التجريـدية والتفـريغية، وفي أغلب الأحيـان تُخفِي أهدافًا إمبريالية ورأسمالية وأبوية. هذه المفاهيم الديمقـراطية للمسـاواة عندمـا تكـون فعَّالة (ومتعـالية، وفقًـا لمنطقهـا الـدارويني الاجتمـاعي) تعمـل من خلال أشكال من الاستيعـاب القمـعي: حيث يُضـمَّن مـا هـو غيـر متسـاوٍ من خلال تطبيعـه، وذلـك في حـد ذاتـه عمل من أعمـال القضـاء علـى السلبي. لكي يصبـح المرء متساويًا كمـا يُفتـرَض، لابـد أن يتخلـص من كل مـا هـو غيـر مُشتهـى وغيـر مرغـوب وغيـر مُستولـى عليـه - التوتـرات والانقسـامات التي تفرزهـا ذاتيةٌ تـرفض التثـاقُف. هذه الأشـكال الديمقـراطية من إقـامة المسـاواة تسـعى إلـى فصـل السـلبي ثـم تضمينـه في الايجـابي والتهامـه من قِبَلِـه. وهي تتـسبَّب في المزيـد من الشقـوق في الذوات المُخضَـعَة حتـى يُفـرض عليهـا التجانُـس والترابـط مع البِنَـى التي تُنتج الانقسامات. إن المحـروم والمشـوَّه - صـاحب الجسـد المستعمَـر والمـصنّف عرقيّـا والمُستغَـل - الذي يسـعى إلـى المسـاواة مـع أولئـك الذين يُحـدِّدون من هـم مساوين لهـم ومن هـم ليسـوا كذلـك، يستحضـر الشَّنيـع في الديمقـراطية الليبـرالية.

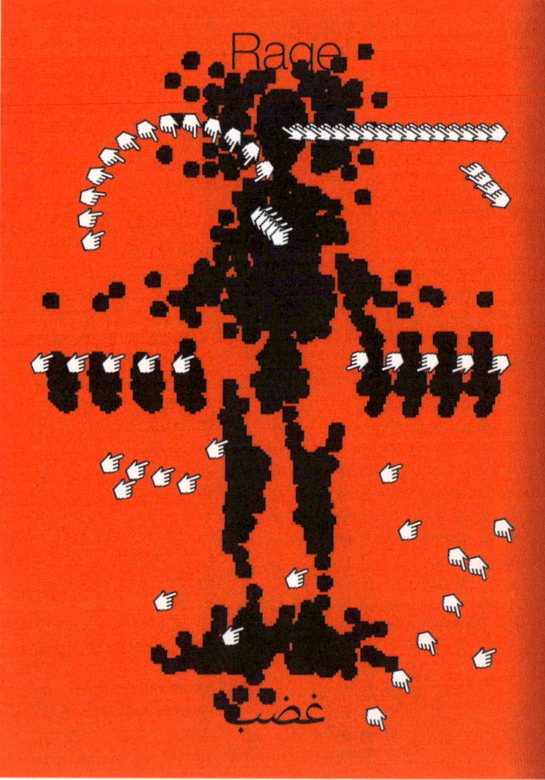

من خلال الكتـابة من الواقـع المـادي والنفسـي لفلسـطين، والتجـارب السيـاسية التي وُلِـدَت من النضـال من أجـل تحريـر الانسـان والجمـاد، والأحيـاء والموتـى[٤]، هنـاك إلحـاح علـى طـرح هذا الـسؤال بجـدية: مـاذا عن الجماليـات التي تتجـاوز مفاهيـم المسـاواة، أو بشـكل أكثـر دقة، مـاذا عن الجماليـات التي تتجـاوز الإيجـابية وتقف

٤
كتبت سهاد ظاهر-ناشف بشكل مُوسَّع عن كيفية احتجاز إسرائيل لجثامين الفلسطينيين كسياسة بدأت مع تأسيس المستعمرة. سواء كانوا مُعتقلين أو مسجونين، يظل الفلسطينيون الذين احتجزوا في السجون الصهيونية هناك بعد وفاتهم. وتوضِّح ظاهر-ناشف كيف تستخدم المستعمرة الاستيطانية الإسرائيلية هذا كتكتيك لتفكيك الجماعة الفلسطينية وكشكل من أشكال إحداث تأثيرات ضارة دائمة على الذاتيات والنفسية السياسية الفلسطينية. انظر/ي

Suhad Daher-Nashif, “Colonial Management of Death: To Be or Not to Be Dead in Palestine.” *Current Sociology 69*, no. 7 (August 28, 2020): 945–62. https://doi.org/10.1177/0011392120948923.

خارجها، الجماليات البروليتارية المعمولة في الإضراب والفعل الثوري والمقاومة، الجماليات التي تتجسّد على الرغم من المَنع. ماذا عن جماليات السلبية والمنقوصة، الجماليات التي هي في الناقص؟ هذه الأسئلة توسّلنا للتفكير فيها بشكل جدلي وضمن التقاليد الفلسفية والسياسية غير المعتادة. يُنظِّر الفنانان باسل عباس وروان أبو رحمة سياسة الكيان «في الناقص» من خلال ممارسة فنية تتكشَّف عند التقاء الصوت والصورة والشعر والأداء.

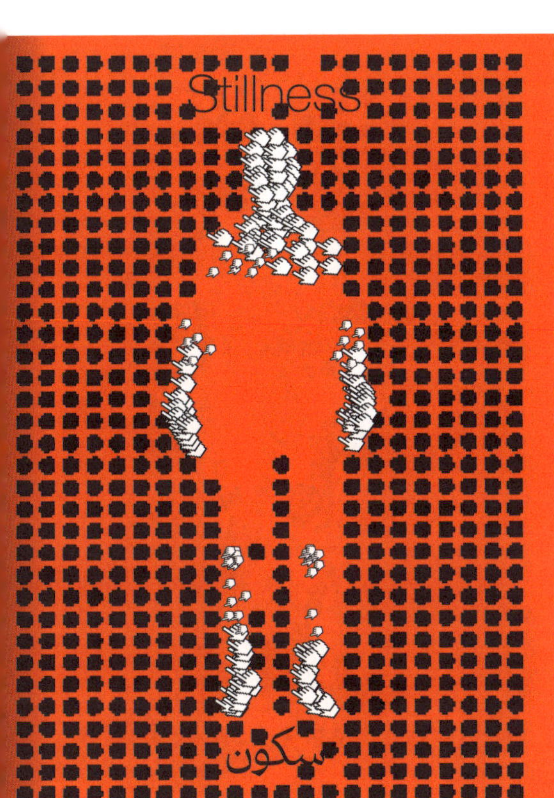

إن عباس وأبو رحمة، من خلال التفكير في السلبية باعتبارها مجال السياسة وليس الانتقال من السلبية (أو أي معادل مفاهيمي[٥]) إلى الإيجابية (رانسيير) أو إدانة السلبية باعتبارها استبعادًا من السياسة لا يُبرهِن إلا على ما هو ضد الإيجابية (أدورنو[٦])، يتصوَّران السلبي باعتباره مكانًا-زمانًا للجِدَّة والإمكانية ويُصرَّان على المكوث فيه، وهي تجربة أشبه بـ«التنفس حيث لا ينبغي لك أن تكون قادرًا على التنفس»[٧]. إن حقيقة جماليات السلبي التي يشير إليها كل من عباس وأبو رحمة، والتي تتجسَّد في أعمالهما الفنية المعاصرة، تتحدث عن المادية الملموسة للعمل الفلسطيني المستخرج والمستغَل والمُخضَع «أن تكون في الناقص هو أن تكون في الدَيْن، في السالِب»[٨]. وهي تتحدث وجدانيًا عن الحضور المادي المنفي والمُنكَر، ليس كحجة كمية أو جنائية، بل كدعوة إلى إيقاظ وتنشيط ذاتية سياسية مكبوتة وكامنة[٩]. أن نُفكِّر في السياسة والجماليات من خلال السلبي، أن نكون «في الناقص» - أن نؤدّي ونُبدع ونتكهَّن ونختلق القصص ونتخيَّل ونُنتج بشكل سلبي - يعني أن نصيغ طريقةً للوجود منغمسة ومضمَّنة في النضال بالكامل مع تجميع إمكانيات العيش والتخيل وإنتاج تجارب اجتماعية حسية و«معرفة غير عادية وغير مسبوقة»[١٠] من خلال حالة الاستبعاد وعلى الرغم منها، أي الانزلاق من الشقوق التي تكسِّر نظام التعرُّف والتعريف[١١].

٥
يعمل رانسيير من خلال فئة اللاإجماع أو «الخلاف» الذي يُشكِّل إنتاجًا لشقوق واضطرابات النظام الحاكم الذي يدير تقديم ورسمنة التجربة الحسية، وتوزيع المحسوس ذاته. ويوضِّح اللاإجماع التفاوتات بين التجارب الحسية داخل المجموعة. انظر/ي

Jacques Rancière, *Dissensus: On Politics and Aesthetics.* (India: Bloomsbury Academic, 2010).

٦
يعمل الجِدَال السلبي عند أدورنو كإدانة أبدية للإيجابي. فالإيجابي، وفقًا لأدورنو، هو ما يلغي التفاصيل والخصوصية والذاتية من خلال التجريد والاستيعاب. والرأسمالية بهذا المعنى هي نظام إيجابي يُضمِّن كل شيء. والسلبي بدوره هو ما يشهد ضد هذا الواقع من خلال التفاصيل ونقد البنية. ومع ذلك، فإن الجِدَال الأدورني مُتحجِّر، وغير مهتم بإيجاد حل، ولا بحل المخطط الجِدَالي. انظر/ي

Theodor Adorno, *Negative Dialectics.* (United Kingdom: Taylor & Francis, 2003).

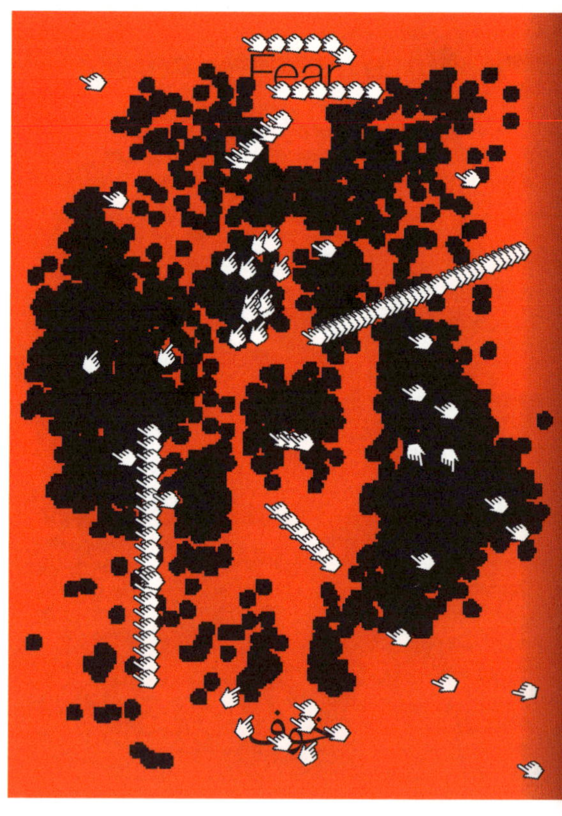

٧
Basel Abbas and Ruanne Abou-Rahme, *May amnesia never kiss us on the mouth*, 2021–, https://mayamnesia.com.

٨
Abbas and Abou-Rahme, *May amnesia*.

٩
Abbas and Abou-Rahme, *May amnesia*.

١٠
Edward W. Said, and Jean Mohr. *After the last sky: Palestinian lives*. New York: Pantheon Books, 1986. 159.

«وهكذا فإن حاجتنا إلى وعي جديد [...] هي حاجتنا إلى شعب تقف تجربته الوطنية [...] عند تلك الحدود المرعبة حيث يتلاشى وجود واختفاء الشعوب في بعضهما البعض، حيث تصبح المقاومة ضرورة، ولكن حيث يوجد أحيانًا أيضًا إدراك متزايد للحاجة إلى معرفة غير عادية، وإلى حد ما، غير مسبوقة».

١١
Abbas and Abou-Rahme, *May amnesia*.

إذا كان عباس وأبو رحمة من منظّري السلبية، فإن جان بودريار من منظّري الإيجابية. في نصٍ كتبه قبل عامين من وفاته، في وقت كان يشعر فيه بخيبة أمل مطلقة تجاه الحركات السياسية والنقد الجذري، قدّم بودريار وصفًا جازمًا للمجتمع المعاصر تُحدِّده الإيجابية الكاملة للسلطة: المحو الكامل للعمل السلبي. بالنسبة إليه، التُهِمَ السلبي وقُلِّص. وما ظهوره من خلال أشكال التنظيم السياسي والنقد الجذري إلّا مفارقة ساخرة، شَبَح. يصف بودريار العلاقة بين الإيجابي والسلبي في العصر النيوليبرالي - عصر حُكم القِيَم والمُصطنَع - بأنها «كارثة جَدَلية»[١٢]. تُقدِّم هذه التصريحات غير المُبهمة من خلال تحليله لانتقال السلطة من مرحلة **السيطرة** إلى مرحلة **الهيمنة**، والمرور الحاسم لرأسمالية ما بعد الحرب من مرحلة الإنتاج إلى مرحلة الاستهلاك. لو كان بودريار على قيد الحياة، لادعى أننا جميعًا متواطئون. وهنا نجد أن جدلية السيد والعبد، و«العمل التاريخي للفكر النقدي، وعلاقة القوى ضد القمع، والذاتية الجذرية ضد الاغتراب، أشياء تقع كلها (تقريبًا) في الماضي»[١٣]. لكن أين يترك تكوين اجتماعي كهذا عمل الناقص في فكر عباس وأبو رحمة؟ الإجابة بسيطة إلى حد ما: في الممارسات اليومية التي تُصرُّ، على الرغم من كل التهديدات بالإبادة أو محاولات الاستيعاب، على إنتاج عمل غير ممسوك، ولغة غير مفهومة، وشكل من أشكال الوجود في الناقص، أي ***جعل السلبي صيرورة***، والتحرر من القيود، والمقاومة من خلال أشكال الرفض في موقف لا تبقى فيه أي خسارة أخرى ممكنة[١٤].

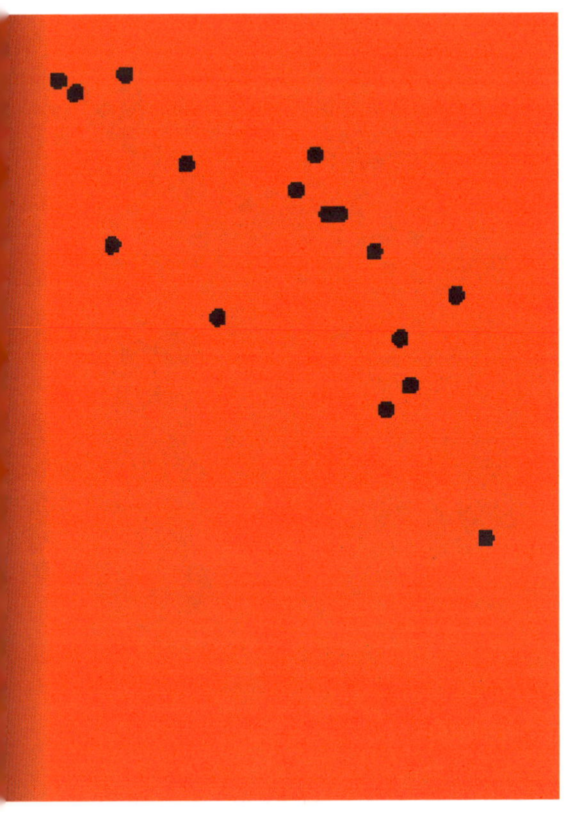

١٢
Jean Baudrillard, *The agony of power.* (South Pasadena, CA: Semiotext(e), 2010), 61.

١٣
Jean Baudrillard, *The agony of power.* (South Pasadena, CA: Semiotext(e), 2010), 60.

١٤
Basel Abbas and Ruanne Abou-Rahme, *Being the negative*, (New York/Palestine: Bilna'es, 2024). 5.

١

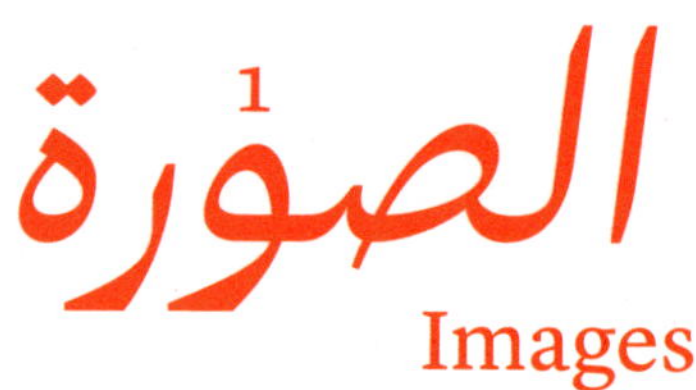

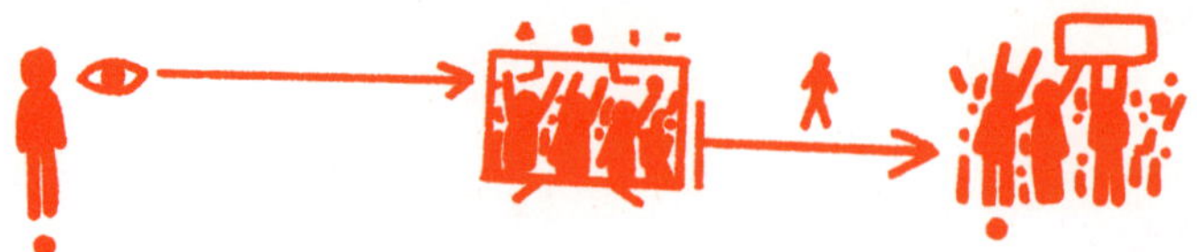

١

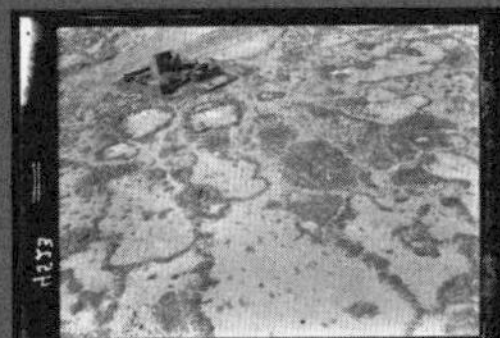

LC-DIG-matpc-15956

٢

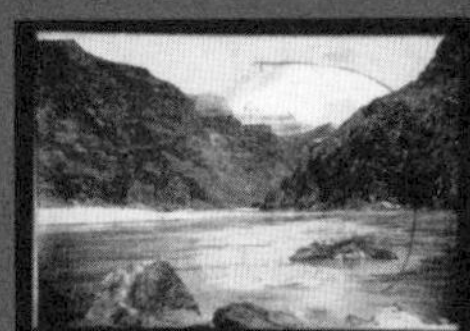

LC-DIG-matpc-15044

٣

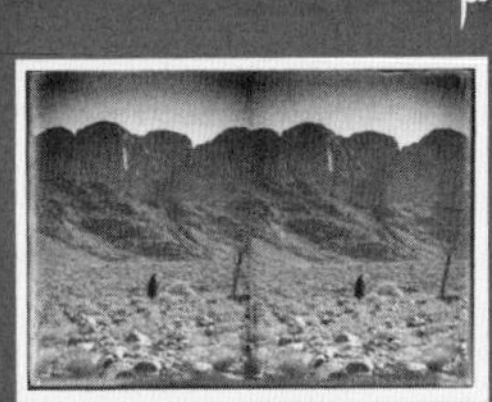

LC-DIG-matpc-02011

٤

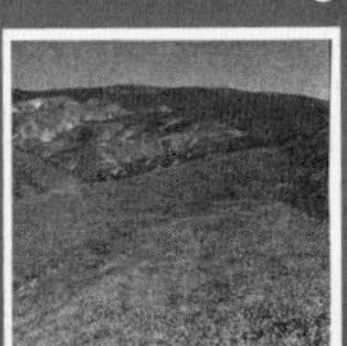

LC-DIG-matpc-15050

٥

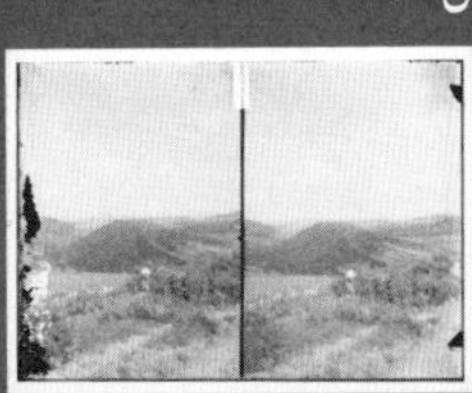

LC-DIG-matpc-10574

١ و
٢ ج.ه.ف.ر
٣ ح.ص.ش
٤ أ.ب.ل.ع
٥ د.ز.ط.ي.ق.م.س.ك.ت

من المتفقّ أن عملية التصوير الشمسي على الألواح الفضية التي أُدخِلَت إلى فرنسا في عام ١٨٣٩ هي أقدم عملية تصوير مسجَّلة تجاريًا. وفي العام نفسه، سُجِّلت أول صورة فوتوغرافية التُقِطَت في فلسطين بهذه العملية التصويرية في القدس. وعلى الرغم من أنها حقيقة مذهلة، إلا أن التداخل يعود إلى التغيرات السياسية والتقنية الاجتماعية والاقتصادية المتنوعة التي كانت تتكشَّف وتتشكَّل في فلسطين في ذلك الوقت (وفي الأعوام التي تلت ذلك) وعلاقتها بكيفية بدء تصوير فلسطين وسكانها الأصليين، الفلسطينيين، ضمن نظام بصري جديد.

وعلى الرغم من أن فلسطين باعتبارها **الأرض المُقدَّسة** تسبق (وبالتأكيد تتخطّى) طريقة التصوير الشمسي على الألواح الفضية، فقد كانت بالفعل موضوعًا لأساليب سابقة لإعادة الإنتاج غير الفوتوغرافي - باتت الحاجة الامبريالية لتصوّر المستعمرة مطلبًا ثقافيًا يُشكِّل التكنولوجيا. لقد استُدعيت الصور الاستعمارية للحياة البرية والعِمارة المقدسة في فلسطين باعتبارها أشياء تُرضي الفانتازيّات المسيحانية. فالصور الخلّابة للتلال والحقول القاحلة كانت بمثابة دعوة لأوروبا للاستيطان و«التخصيب». كان توثيق الحياة الفلسطينية بمثابة توهم مستقبلي للحياة الاستعمارية التي **يمكن** تأسيسها **هناك**. تم أخذ لقطات جوية للقرى والغابات والمسطَّحات المائية بغرض توفير مصدر جمالي من البيانات للبريطانيين والصهاينة، وأساس بصري للاستيطان والإدارة ورسم الحدود والعسكرة وإدارة السكان. وأنتجَ هذا النوع من التصوير «بورتريهات» للذات الأصلانية المستعمرة عبر مُحدِّدات استعمارية تتّسم بإضفاء الغرابة، والتصنيفات العرقية، والمراقبة، والمعلوماتية. كان ذلك كلّه عبارة عن أجهزة في طور التكوين، إما رَفَدَت التطور الفوتوغرافي أو رَفَدها النظام البصري الذي استحضره التصوير الفوتوغرافي.

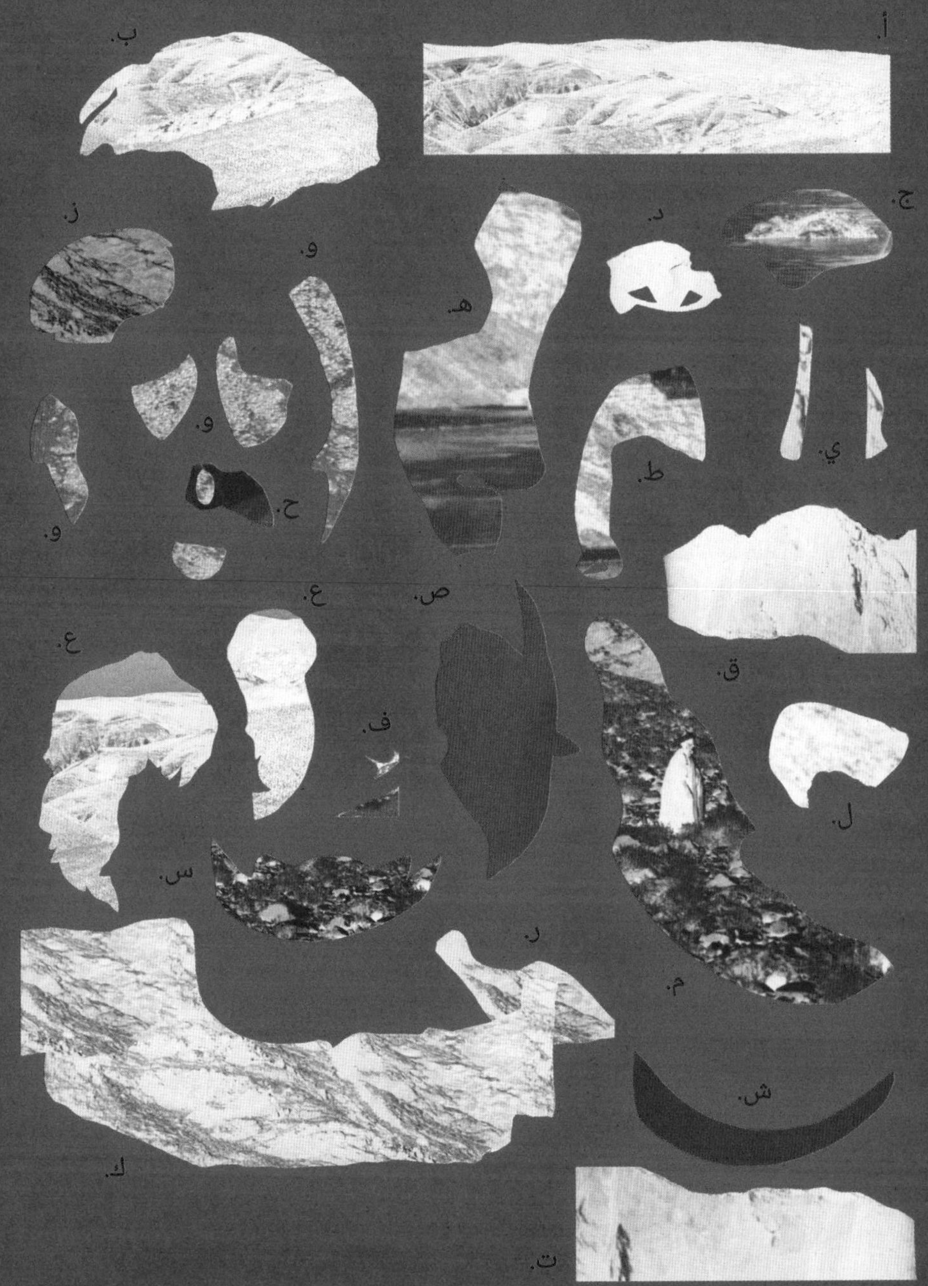
أ.
ب.
ج.
د.
ز.
و.
هـ.
و.
ي.
ط.
ح.
و.
ص.
ع.
ع.
ق.
ف.
ل.
س.
ر.
م.
ش.
ك.
ت.

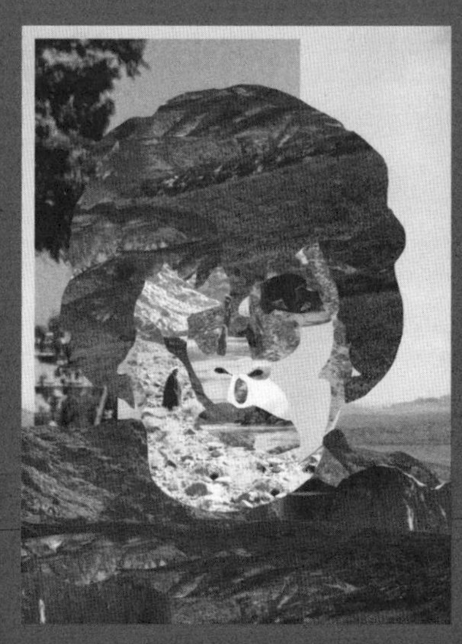

ماذا نفعل إذًا بالصور التي تلتقطنا؟ هل نحرقها بشكل احتفالي في فعل خُروج جماعي من نظام بصري مُستبد؟ وإذا أشعلنا فيها النار، فهل سنحترق أيضًا؟ وإذا كان بوسعنا القضاء على هذه الصور، فماذا يعني أن نكون من دون صورة، إذ بمجرد التقاطها، هل يمكننا الهروب؟ هل نستطيع أن ننسلّ بعيدًا، وإذا كان الأمر كذلك، فما هو الشيء الذي على المحك؟ يمكن للمرء أن ينتهز هذه الفرصة لرواية وإعادة سرد العنف الاستعماري والعرقي والرأسمالي للصورة، لكن العديد من المفكِّرين فعلوا ذلك من دون كلل وبطرق من غير الضروري الزيادة عليها. لقد أدى وصول التصوير الفوتوغرافي وفي الواقع الحداثة نفسها إلى فلسطين، سواء بفرضٍ من جانب الاستعمار البريطاني والصهيوني أو برعاية من جانب البرجوازيين العرب في القرنين التاسع عشر والعشرين، إلى ظهور أشكال جديدة من الإكراه والهيمنة التكنولوجية والاجتماعية والذاتية. ومع ذلك، فقد أنتجت هذه التكنولوجيا أشكالًا سياسية للوجود والمشاركة في إطار الحداثة و إعادة هيكلتها وبنائها أيضًا. هذا هو عمل السلبي في الذاتيات السياسية: صياغة تكتيكات واستراتيجيات سياسية غير مسبوقة وأساليب حياة حديثة، وإنتاج تجارب سياسية حسية تفتح، بالتقنيات الحديثة نفسها، حقائق زمنية بديلة. وباعتبارهم ذوات الحداثة الاستعمارية، يواصل الفلسطينيون المناورة والتحوُّل وإنتاج طرق جديدة للعيش والوجود على الرغم من أنظمة العنف هذه، حيث يعيدون تشكيل أنفسهم باستمرار بحثًا عن الحياة في الموت.

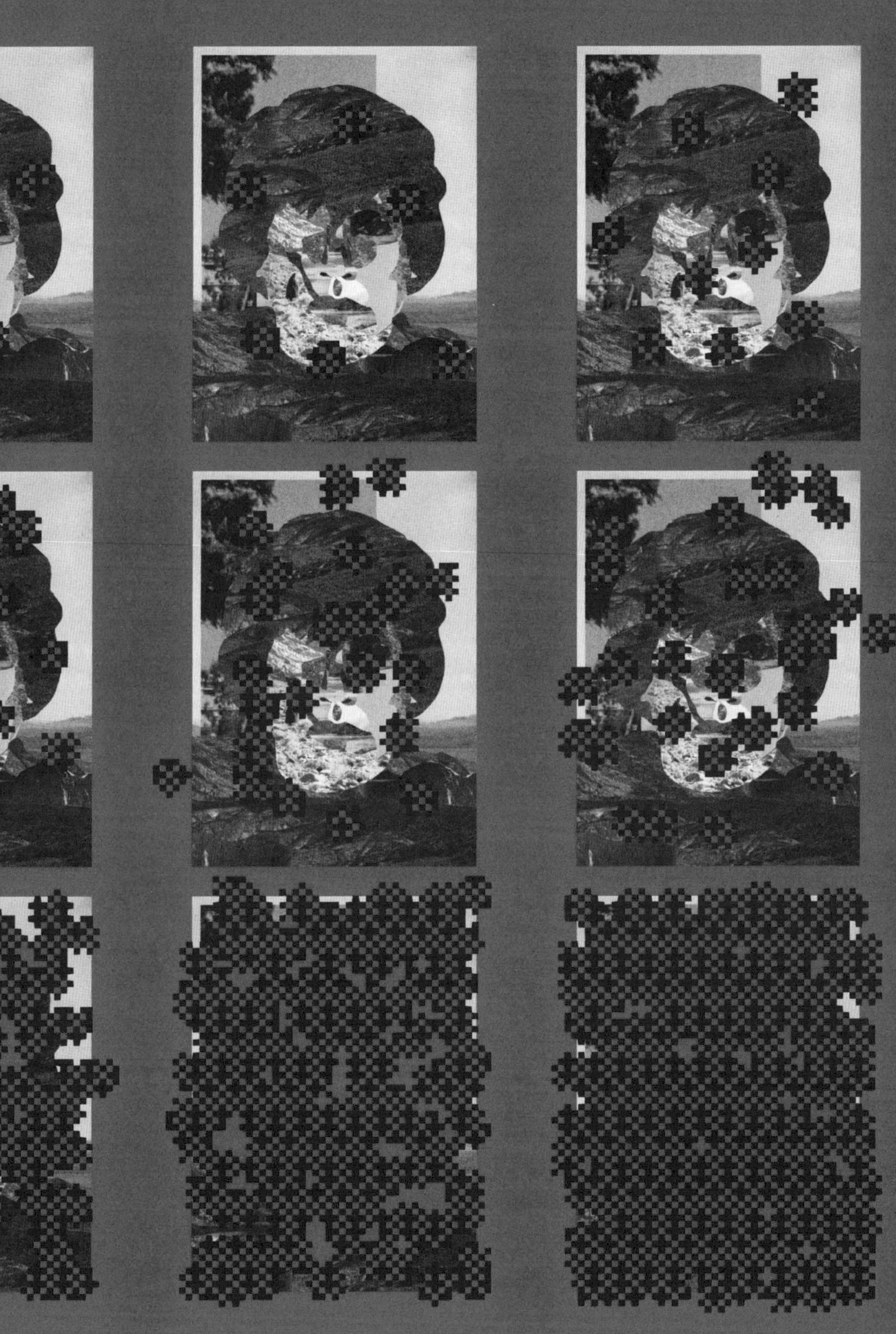

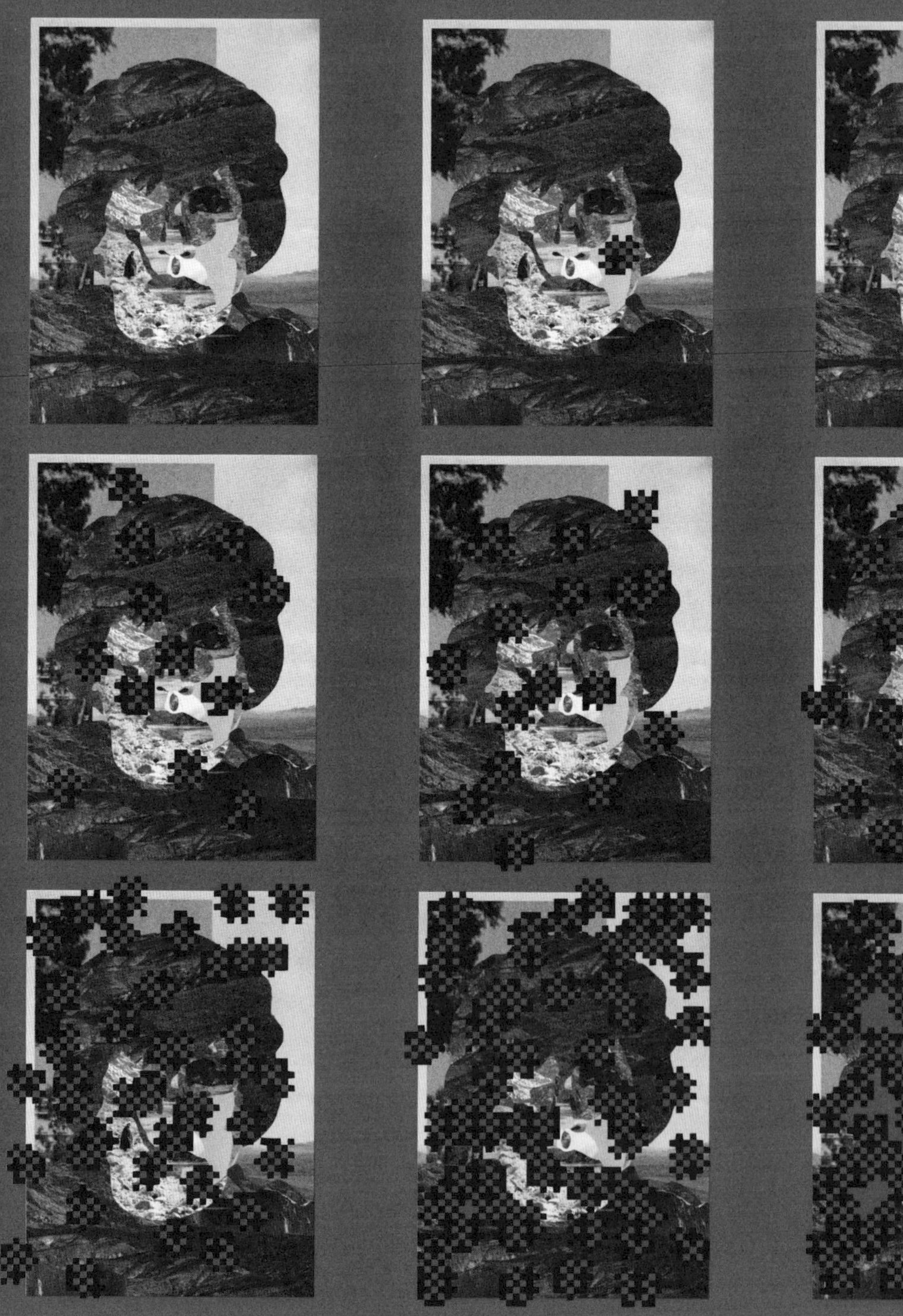

أريد أن أكون تلك الصورة

خلال هبّة الكرامة الفلسطينية في أيار/مايو ٢٠٢١، كنا تحت سحر الصور. لم يكن من الواضح ما إذا كانت هذه الصور تحاول التقاطنا ونحن نثور، أم أننا من يحاول التقاطها وهي تهرب. لمدة أشهر، سيطر نوع معيّن من الصور على مجال رؤيتنا. احتلّ العالم الافتراضي عوالمنا النفسية من خلال صور لامادية. إذ أصبحت هذه الصور مطبوعة في خيالنا، واشترعَت معانٍ جديدة في نظامنا الدلالي، وصاغت دلالات جديدة لما هو ممكن، ولطبيعة الواقع الذي يمكن أن تدل عليه صورة معينة، وكيف تؤكد دلالة مثل هذا الواقع المتخيل ماديته[١٥]. تُعلِن هذه الصور عن الواقع المحتمل الذي يمكن أن تستحضره صورة معينة، حتى لو كان ذلك بشكل عابر، وتكشف هذه الصورة اللامادية كيف يُحوِّل استحضار *ما يمكن أن يكون ممكنًا* إلى قوة ملموسة في حياتنا. كانت الصور المتداولة عبر الإنترنت رقمية ولامادية، مثل صور الفِكر، على نحو يُتيح لنا إسقاط فلسطين التي أردنا رؤيتها عليها، بينما تركت أيضًا أثرًا لكيفية تكشُّف فلسطين المنشودة هذه داخلها. مثل طيف أو شَبَح مستقبلي أو هاجِس، أغرتنا هذه الصور بالدخول إلى العوالم التي سمحت لنا بفتحها، وشَرعت لنا آفاقًا جديدة في مجال الرؤية، وأتاحت لنا إمكانيةً كانت مستحيلة في السابق[١٦]. وقد شاهدنا مرارًا صورًا لمستوطنين يقتحمون

١٥
Émile Benveniste, *Problems in General Linguistics.* (United States: University of Miami Press, 1971), 45.

١٦
في تحليلها لنقد إميل بنفنست للسانيات السوسورية، كتبت منى بنيامين كيف أن كلمة «خيال» في اللغة العربية «مُشتقَّة من الفعل الجذري «خالَ» (بالإنكليزية، الفعل الماضي thought)، وقد عرَّف «معجم اللغة العربية الحديثة» الخيال بأنه «صورة باقية في النفس بعد غيبة المحسوس عنها، الصورة الشخصيَّة التي تمثّل المعنى المجرّد تمثيلًا واضحًا»، والخيال مرادف أيضًا لكلمتي «طيف» و«ظِل» [...] كلمة خيال مبنية على الفعل الجذري «خالَ» وبالتالي لا تنفصل عنه، وكما يقول لنا بنفنست، فإن «الفكرة (thought) ليست مادة تمنحها اللغةُ شكلًا، لأنه لا يمكن في أي وقت أن نتخيل هذا «الوعاء» فارغًا من محتوياته، ولا أن نتخيل «المحتويات» مستقلة عن «وعائها»». أتوجَّه بالشكر إلى منى بنيامين على مشاركتي مسودتها غير المنشورة، وإلى نور عنّان على تحدِّي حجتي من خلال العلاقة بين صور الفِكر والصور الرقمية.

منازل فلسطينيين في القدس ويافا ومسافر يطا، كمشاهد لنزوحنا المستمر. إن النضال وطني، لكن الواقع الاستعماري في فلسطين يعزل مراكز المواجهة، ويجعلها تبدو مُشتّتة، حيث يُشكل كل موقع منها عالمًا مصغرًا يقنعنا بأن عنف المستعمرة الاستيطانية **هنا** أو **هناك** يختلف عن المستوطنات في بقية الأرض - لكن فقط إذا سمحنا بذلك. وفي ظل هذا التكتيك الاستعماري المُشرذِم، منحتنا صور العنف القمعي إمكانية الوصول الحصري إلى حشود فلسطين، على نحو يسمح لنا بتجاوز التخطيط الاستيطاني لبلادنا، حتى ولو كان ذلك افتراضيًا. وفي لحظة ما من أيار/مايو ٢٠٢١، طغت على تلك الصور ذاتها صور أخرى ذات طبيعة مختلفة: فقد حلّت مكان صور المستوطنين وهم يغادرون قُرانا ومدننا وبلداتنا التي كانوا قد استوطنوها صور العائلات التي طُردت من مسافر يطا. وفجأة، صَوَّرَت الشوارع التي صُوِّرَت وتُخُيِّلَت على أنها مخصصة لليهود فقط عودة الوجود المكبوت للفلسطينيين، الذين أخذوا يركضون في مساحات لا يُسمح لهم بالتواجد فيها. وتحولت صور الأحياء القديمة في عكا إلى ضواح إسرائيلية ساحلية تكشفت على شاشاتنا كمساحات يجب استعادتها من مخالب الاستيطان وخصخصة الاستعمار.

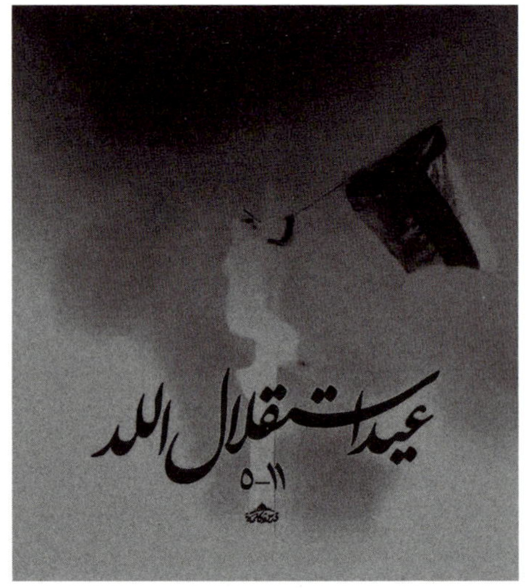

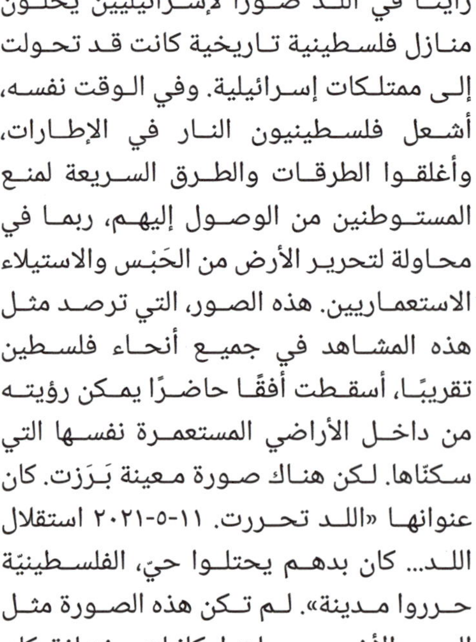

رأينا في اللد صورًا لإسرائيليين يخلون منازل فلسطينية تاريخية كانت قد تحولت إلى ممتلكات إسرائيلية. وفي الوقت نفسه، أشعل فلسطينيون النار في الإطارات، وأغلقوا الطرقات والطرق السريعة لمنع المستوطنين من الوصول إليهم، ربما في محاولة لتحرير الأرض من الحَبْس والاستيلاء الاستعماريين. هذه الصور، التي ترصد مثل هذه المشاهد في جميع أنحاء فلسطين تقريبًا، أسقطت أفقًا حاضرًا يمكن رؤيته من داخل الأراضي المستعمرة نفسها التي سكنّاها. لكن هناك صورة معينة بَرَزت. كان عنوانها «اللد تحررت. ١١-٥-٢٠٢١ استقلال اللد... كان بدهم يحتلوا حيّ، الفلسطينيّة حرروا مدينة». لم تكن هذه الصورة مثل الصور الأخرى. حملت إمكانات مختلفة. كان

هناك شيء شهواني (ليبيدي) فيها، الطريقة التي تم بها العمل عليها، والأداء الذي ظهر فيها، والاسلوب الذي تم تداولها فيه. وعلى الرغم من انتشارها على منصات وسائل التواصل (التوسُّط) الاجتماعي المشبعة بحكم إيجابية رأس المال، فإن الصورة حافظت على سلبية عابرة تحدَّت الاستيلاء عليها. فما عرضته على المشاهدين ينفي منطق الاستهلاك. قامت تلك الصورة لرجل ملثَّم تسلق أعلى عمود إنارة وهو يحمل علم فلسطين والذي غرسه في شقوق ثَقَبها بالعمود في فعل من أفعال التحدي. وبعد التقاط المشهد، نقش أحدهم على الصورة بخط عربي عبارة «عيد استقلال اللد. ١١ أيار». ومنذ اجتياحها للإنترنت، بدأت تنتشر بسرعة. لم نعرف ما إذا كان علينا أن نصدقها أم لا، لكن الإمكانية التي طرحتها سمحت لنا بتجاوز قيود واقعنا الاستعماري. ما أشارت إليه هذه الصورة كان نداءً - كما قال المفكّر الراحل وليد دقّة - من زمن مواز[١٧]. وبصرف النظر عن المشهد نفسه، وسواء تحررت اللد بالفعل أم لا، فقد جسدت الصورة خيالًا ثوريًا جماعيًا في شكل جمالي الذي انتشر على نطاق واسع. عبَّرت الصورة عن إمكانية مُعلَّقة في زمن بعيد مُنتظَر كحَدَث قد تبلوَرَ في الحاضر. قام الرجل الملثَّم بفعل تمرد مستخدمًا جسده، ثم التُقِطَ هذا الفعل، وحُرِّرت الصورة الخام وتم تداولها لتوصيل واقع جديد - بين الفانتازيا والإنجاز الملموس - للتحرُّر الفلسطيني. وصلت إلينا هذه الصورة الليبيدية وحرَّكتنا. والسؤال الذي تردَّد في أذهاننا وعلى ألسنتنا كان: «إذا كانت اللد قد أعلنت استقلالها، فما الذي يمنع عين قينيا أو رفح أو حيفا أو جنين من إعلان استقلالها؟». ماذا لو كُنَّا نحن الرجلَ الملثَّم، ماذا لو كان أداؤه أدائنا، ماذا لو فعلنا ما فعله؟

«المحاكاة السياسية»[١٨] هو المصطلح الذي استخدمته جين جاينز لوصف العلاقة بين المتفرجين الذين يشاهدون لقطات وثائقية للثورات السياسية والأجساد التي صُوِّرَت في تلك اللقطات وهي تؤدِّي أعمالًا سياسية. كتبت جاينز: «[...] تتعلَّق المحاكاة السياسية بإنتاج التأثُّر في صور النضال التقليدية ومن خلالها: الجثث الملطخة بالدماء والحشود المتظاهرة والشرطة الغاضبة. لكن من الواضح أن مثل هذه الصور لن يكون لها صدى من دون السياسة، السياسة التي تُنظِّرَ على أنها وعي، وفي الماركسية على أنها وعي طبقي... المعضلة هنا أنه في حين أننا لا نريد قط أن نقترح أن عملية تطوير الوعي الطبقي لاإرادية أو قائمة على التقليد، فإننا بحاجة إلى الاعتراف بأنه في

أَسْـر الأغـاني الجمـاعية، وفي خِضَـم المعـركة، وفي الإجهـاد البـدني والمقـاومة الجسـدية، من المؤكـد أنـه قـد يكـون هنـاك في بـعض الأحيـان جـانب من اللاإرادي، جـانب «يفعـل فعلـه» فـوق الـوعي المُسيِّـس». علـى الرغـم من أن سؤال جـاينز يفحـص قـدرة صنـاعة الأفلام الوثـائقية علـى إحـداث التغييـر السيـاسي، أو علـى الأقـل الصحـوة السيـاسية التي تُشـكِّل في حـد ذاتهـا تحـولًا من حـالة إلـى أخـرى، فإن الـسؤال يظـل قائمًـا في واقعنـا المعاصـر المشبـع بصـور النضـال التي تتـكشَّف علـى شاشـاتنا في وقت حدوثهـا. وهنـاك بالفعـل فـارق بين الصـورة الوثـائقية الثـورية والصـورة المـوثقة التي التُقِـطَت في وقت الثـورة، ولـكن هذا الفـارق لـه علاقة باقتصاديـات التـداول، ومـادية الإنتـاج، أو بعبـارة أخـرى، جماليـات وسياسـات الصـور وعمـلية إضفـاء الطابـع الجمـالي علـى الصـور السيـاسية[١٩].

إن إطـار المحـاكاة الذي اقترحتـه جـاينز لفهـم سياسـات الـوعي الجمـاعي التي تُيسِّـرها الصـور مقنـع لـسببين. الأول هـو أنه في عصر إعـادة الإنتاج، تُقدِّم المحـاكاة حلًا للتضاعُـف يتجـاوز مفاهيـم الإنتـاج الرأسـمالي. ففي الرأسـمالية، تُنتَـج الرغبـات ويُعـاد إنتاجهـا للاستهلاك والإخضـاع الضمني. نريـد أن نشتـري مـا يشتريـه الآخـرون، ونستهلـك مـا يستهلكـه الآخـرون، ونؤدِّي العمـل المستغَّل لنكـون مرغـوبين مثـل الآخـرين. إن المحـاكاة هي الـرغبة التي تحـاكي رغبـات الآخـرين ـ وليـس الـرغبة المعـاد إنتاجهـا، وهـو مـا يـعني أن شـكلها فـارغ من المضمـون. و«المحـاكاة السيـاسية»، بحـسب جـاينز، هي الـرغبة التي تحـاكي الرغبـات التخـريبية للآخـرين. وعلـى الرغـم من الفـراغ والشـكل الفـارغ لتلـك الـرغبة، فإن الشـكل يظـل خطيـرًا ومعاديًـا لنظـام السـلطة. والمحـاكاة في لحظـات الاضطرابـات السيـاسية تُقـدِّم ارتباطًـا مباشـرًا بين الجماليـات والتجـربة النفـسية الاجتمـاعية. وهذه الـعلاقة بين رغبة الجسـد المتفـرج في أداء فعـل مماثـل للجسـد الملتقـط في الصـورة تستـحق الفحـص والتـدقيق.

١٩
Mary Jirmanus Saba, "What's the Use of a Strike Archive?" *Critical Times* 5, no. 3 (December 1, 2022): 663–87.
https://doi.org/10.1215/26410478-10030274.

١٧
وليد دقّة، «السيطرة بالزمن»، أوان، ١٦ حزيران/يونيو، ٢٠٢١.
https://www.awanmedia.net/article/6046.

١٨
Political Mimesis.

إن التفسير التحليلي النفسي التاريخي البارز للفن، أو للشكل الجمالي الذي يحدث في موضوع التحليل النفسي، يُفهَم من خلال التسامي[٢٠] الذي يوفر «للدافع»[٢١]، كما قال لاكان، «إشباعًا مختلفًا عن هدفه»[٢٢]. إن التسامي في الفن، في جوهره، عملية تُنتِج القيمة بين غرض الرغبة - قيمة لا يمكن تبادلها، قيمة بلا وظيفة وفقًا لمنطق التبادل الرأسمالي. وعندما نعود إلى مفهوم المحاكاة السياسية، تتشكل هذه العلاقة النفسية المتخيَّلة بين الجسد المتفرِّج والجسد الذي يؤدِّي أعمالًا سياسية، وهي علاقة ما بين قيَّم مُجرَّدة. إن قيمة الرغبة المتسامية المُعبَّر عنها في شكل جمالي والمُجسَّدة بواسطة الجسد المؤدِّي في الصورة تُشكِّل علاقة بقيمة جديدة تنتجها رغبة متسامية مُعبَّر عنها في المحاكاة السياسية. ولأن كلتا القيمتين عبارة عن أشكال بلا مضمون، فإنهما تتمتعان بصفة إتاحة الاستخدام لتحقيق أهداف سياسية ثورية. إن المكبوتين قادرون على استخدام الصور المتداولة على منصات التواصل الاجتماعي - المنتجة من خلال أنظمة المراقبة والتعريف التكنولوجية الاجتماعية لأغراض التراكم الرأسمالي والقمع السياسي - وتغيير أهداف استخدامها بشكل يتوافق مع أغراض سياسية تتعارض مع ظروفها الإنتاجية.

٢٠
Sublimation.

٢١
Drive.

٢٢
في أكثر صِيَغه اللاكانية تطورًا، يُعرَّف التسامي بأنه عملية تنطوي على السجلات الثلاثة للاوعي: الخيالي، والرمزي، والواقعي. يكتب لاكان: «إن التسامي الذي يوفِّر للدافع إشباعًا مختلفًا عن هدفه - وهو الهدف الذي لا يزال يُعرَّف باعتباره هدفه الطبيعي - هو على وجه التحديد ما يكشف عن الطبيعة الحقيقية للدافع من حيث هو ليس محض غريزة، وإنما له علاقة بالشيء بحد ذاته، بالشيء بقدر ما هو متميز عن الغرض».

(Jacques Lacan, *The Ethics of Psychoanalysis, 1959-1960: The Seminar of Jacques Lacan, Book VII.* (United Kingdom: Routledge, 1999), 111).

يفسر لاكان الأمر باعتباره تجاوزًا للغرض الخيالي للشيء الحقيقي عبر الرمزي: «رفع الغرض إلى منزلة الشيء».

(Jacques Lacan, *The Ethics of Psychoanalysis, 1959-1960: The Seminar of Jacques Lacan, Book VII.* (United Kingdom: Routledge, 1999), 112).

في حالة العمل الفني، فإن صورة الواقعي هي التي لا يمكن تمثيلها قط، ولكن يمكن استدعاؤها. ومنزلة «الشيء»، التي هي ليست الشيء نفسه، هي الرغبة الجنسية (الخيالي) التي ترتفع إلى شكل جمالي (الواقعي) يُصاغ من خلال الرمزي.

٢٣
نشر النص أصلًا بالفارسية على موقع
harasswatch.com
يوم الأربعاء 28 أيلول/سبتمبر 2022، ويمكن الوصول إليه عبر الإنترنت من خلال هذا الرابط:
https://bit.ly/3AWsNk9.

ونُشرت الترجمة الإنكليزية الأولى التي قام بها علي رضا دوستدار، مع مدخلات من المؤلف، على «جدلية» تحت عنوان

"Figuring a Women's Revolution: Bodies Interacting with their Images"

ويمكن الوصول إليها عبر الإنترنت من خلال هذا الرابط:
https://bit.ly/3XCaI3O.

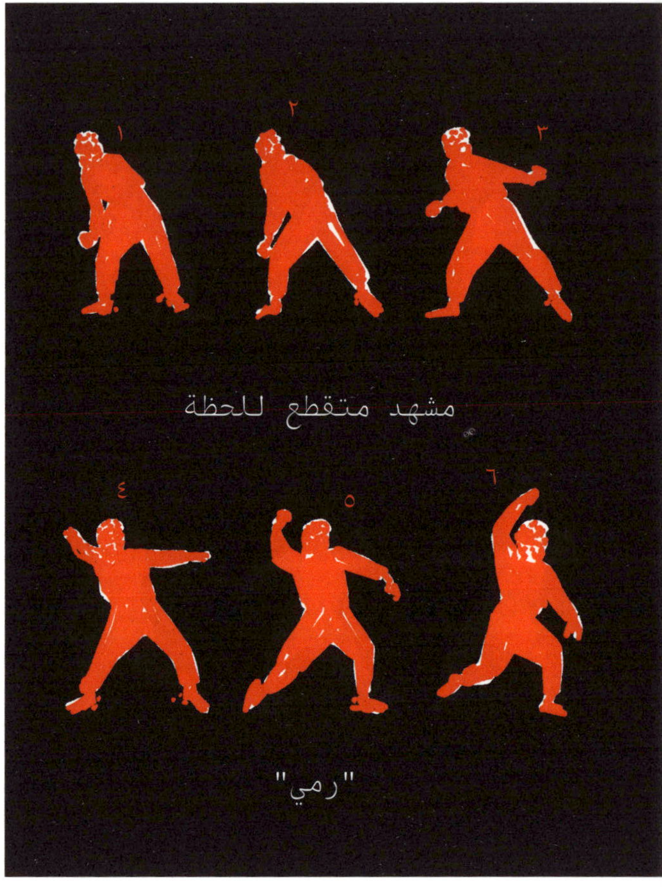

هذه الملاحظة ليست مجرد تجربة حسية تم تحويلها إلى تجريد فكري، حيث قدّم نشطاء وفنانون، وغيرهم ممن وجدوا أنفسهم في قلب حَدَث سياسي من دون تخطيط مسبق، تأملات مستمرة تشهد على هذه التجربة النفسية. فعلى سبيل المثال هناك مادّة متداولة نُشرت تحت الاسم المستعار «ل» والتي ظهرت لأول مرة على المنصة النسوية اليسارية الإيرانية التابعة لمجموعة «هاراس ووتش» خلال هبّة عام ٢٠٢٢ في إيران[٢٣]. وتتميز المقالة بما حفّز كتابتها: «محاولة لفهم حدسٍ وُلد من اختبار هوّة فاصلة ما بين مشاهدة صور وفيديوهات الاحتجاجات عبر الإنترنت، والتواجد في الشارع. هو جهد لتفسير «الماس الكهربائي» الحاصل في الثغرة المفتوحة ما بين الحيّز الافتراضي والواقع في الشارع في هذه اللحظة التاريخية»[٢٤].

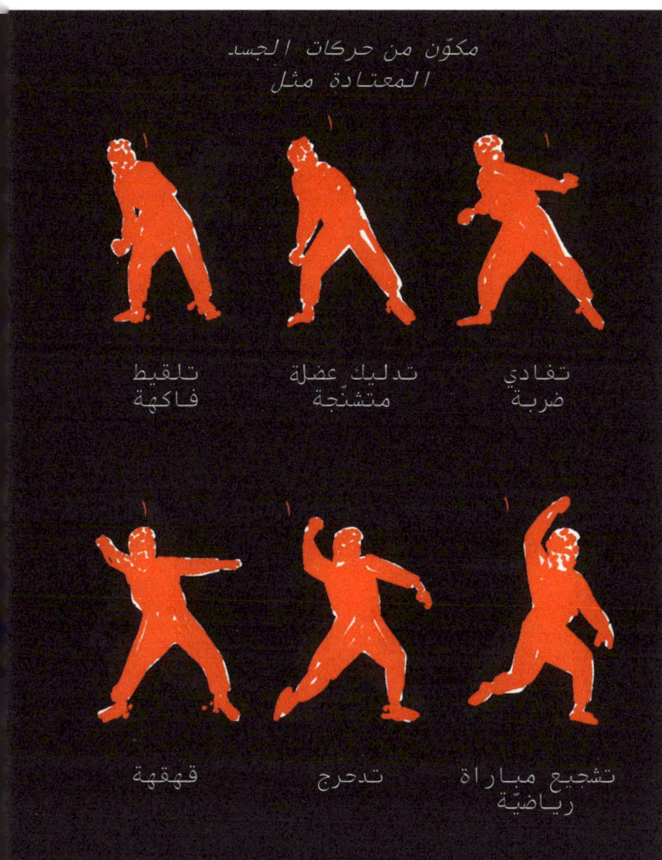

٢٥ Bloch, Ernst. *The Heritage of Our Times*. Germany: Polity Press, 2015.

في مقالها «ثورة نسويّة تتشكّل: الأجساد تتفاعل مع صورها»، تكتب «ل» عن تجربتها في متابعة الاحتجاجات عبر صور وفيديوهات للثورة، صور أجساد تحرق أوشحة، وتُخرِّب ممتلكات للدولة، وتتعرَّض للضرب، وتجربة العثور على نفسها في الشوارع تعيد خلق المشاهد نفسها التي شاهدتها. تشهد روايتها على كيف أن نوعًا معينًا من المعرفة، أو ذاكرة كامنة مخزنة في الجسد، تحفّز رد فعل يتحرك بشكل أسرع من ذلك الذي يفرضه العقل. روايتها مذهلة لأنها تُعبِّر عن المحاكاة كشكل جمالي يستحضر رغبات من اللاوعي. تشاهد صور الاحتجاجات والثورة وتجد نفسها تُعيد خلق المشاهد الملتقطة فيها بسبب رغبة في تقليدها. تتأمّل «ل» أيضًا كيف يتشكّل زمن الثورة عندما ينفتح الزمن وتتصادم الزمانيّات. تتحرك أجسادنا على نحو أسرع منا، وننهض دائمًا متأخرين لثورة يُعاد إنتاجها مرارًا كشيء مُنتَظَر[٢٥].

٢٦
Ernst Bloch, "Nonsynchronism and the Obligation to Its Dialectics." Translated by Mark Ritter. New German Critique, no. 11 (1977): 22. https://doi.org/10.2307/487802.

٢٧
L., Figuring a Women's Revolution.

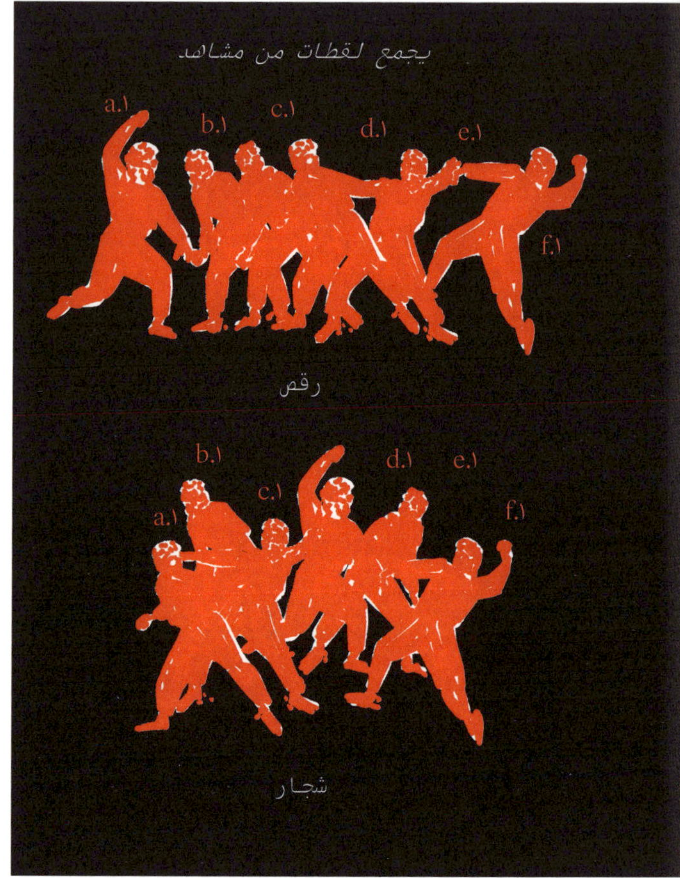

نجد في هذا التأمل صدى لملاحظة إرنست بلوخ حول اللاتزامن: «لا يتواجد كل الناس في اللحظة الآنية نفسها. يبدون كذلك خارجيًا فقط، بحكم الحقيقة أنه يمكن رؤيتهم جميعًا اليوم. لكن هذا لا يعني أنهم يعيشون الوقت نفسه مع بعضهم البعض»[٢٦]. وهذا يستدعي التدقيق في النفس في ظل مثل هذه التحولات والمعاملات.

تكتب «ل»: «قُلّصت المسافة بيني وبين الصور التي جذبتني واستولت على رغباتي، حتى أصبحتُ أنا نفسي تلك الصور. رأيت نفسي فجأةً وسط حلقة أحرق أحجبة، كما لو أنّنا كنّا دائمًا نحرق الأحجبة [...] أدى جسدي من دون وعي تلك الأشياء التي رأيت المحتجات الأخريات يفعلنها. [...] كان الاختلاف الملموس بين هذا الاحتجاج والاحتجاجات التي عشتها من قبل هو الانتقال من «حركة الحشد» إلى «خلق

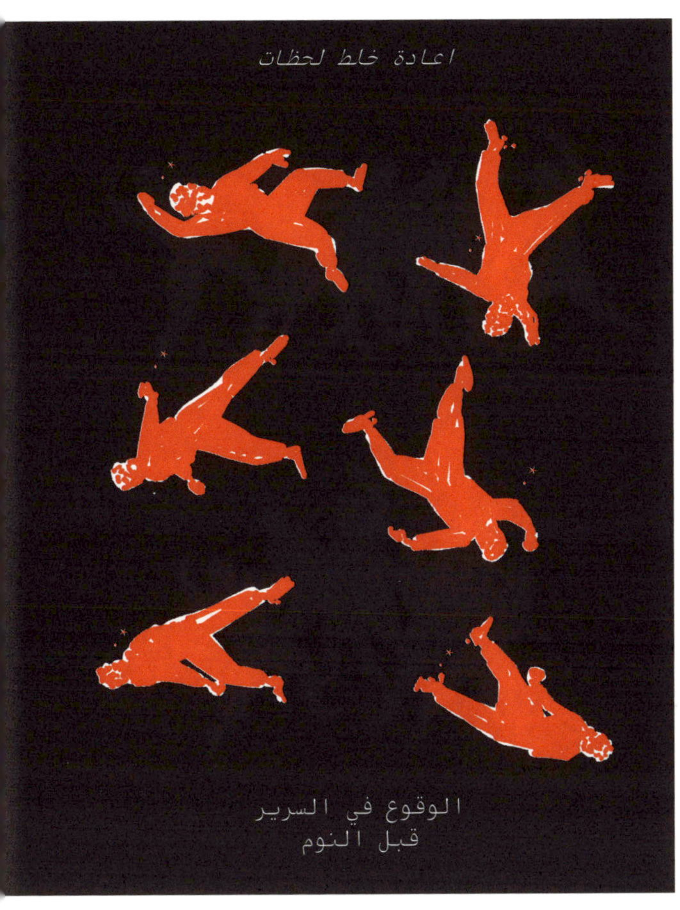

موقف»»[٢٧]. تُيسِّر هذه التجربة النفسية وتُجسِّد من خلال الجماليات، من خلال الحِسِّي والحَاسِّي. تشهد رواية «ل» أيضًا على واقع متناقض معين للتنظيم السياسي في العصر النيوليبرالي: إن الانتقال الذي تتحدَّث عنه من «حركة الحشد» إلى «خلق موقف» يُعلِن عن واقع تجمُّع مُلبْرَل ومجزَّأ في حالة من عدم القدرة على تنظيم نفسه ككتلة واحدة. لكن رواية «ل» تشرح أيضًا كيف يجد هذا التجمُّع نفسه، على نحو لاإرادي تقريبًا، في شكل كتلة من الأفراد المنخرطين في نشاط سياسي تخريبي. فالرغبات الذاتية تُخدَّر وتُلتَقَط، وتُحتجَز كرهينة من قِبَل أنظمة وساطة تكنولوجية اجتماعية، وفي الوقت نفسه، في لحظة سياسية، تتشكَّل كتلة غير متعمَّدة على الرغم من اللبرَلَة[٢٨]. والواقع أن الطبيعة المتأصِّلة للرغبات النفسية التي تُعرَّف بـ«النقص» وموضوعات الرغبة التي تتشكَّل من خلال الاغتراب هي

٢٨
Byung-Chul Han, *Psychopolitics: Neoliberalism and New Technologies of Power*. (United Kingdom: Verso Books, 2017).

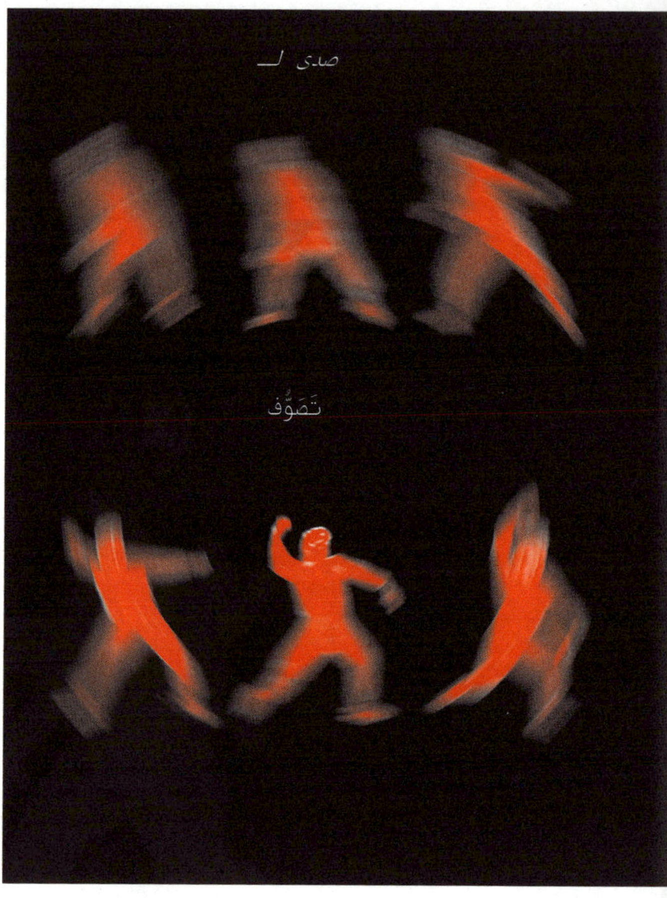

التي تُقـدِّم لنـا هذا الانفتـاح الجذري. ويتجلـى هذا الانفتـاح من خلال النظـام الجمـالي، وفي هذه الحـالة، من خلال تضاعُف الصـور السيـاسية للثـورة والمواجـهة وتجـاوز الحـدود التي كانت تعتبـر في السـابق غيـر قابـلة للتجـاوز. وتؤكـد رواية «ل» في عـام ٢٠٢٢، عنـد قراءتهـا مقـارنة بـروايـة الفلسـطينيين في عـام ٢٠٢١، علـى الطـرق التي انخـرط بهـا الفلسـطينيون في تقاليـد جمـالية من الثـورة تـسبق الواقـع الاستعمـاري المعاصـر وتقنياتـه.

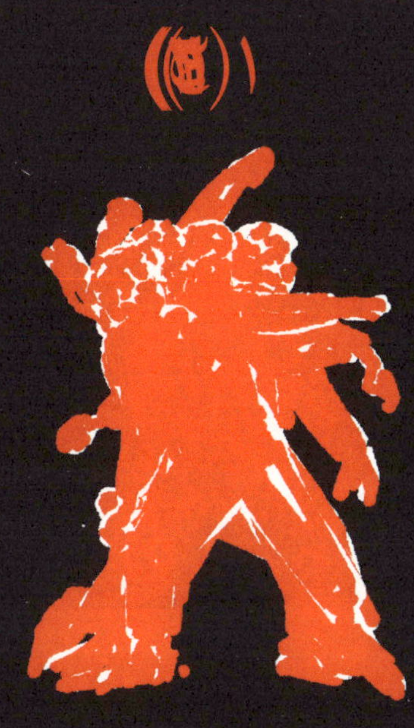

مشهد متراكم للحظة

"رمي"

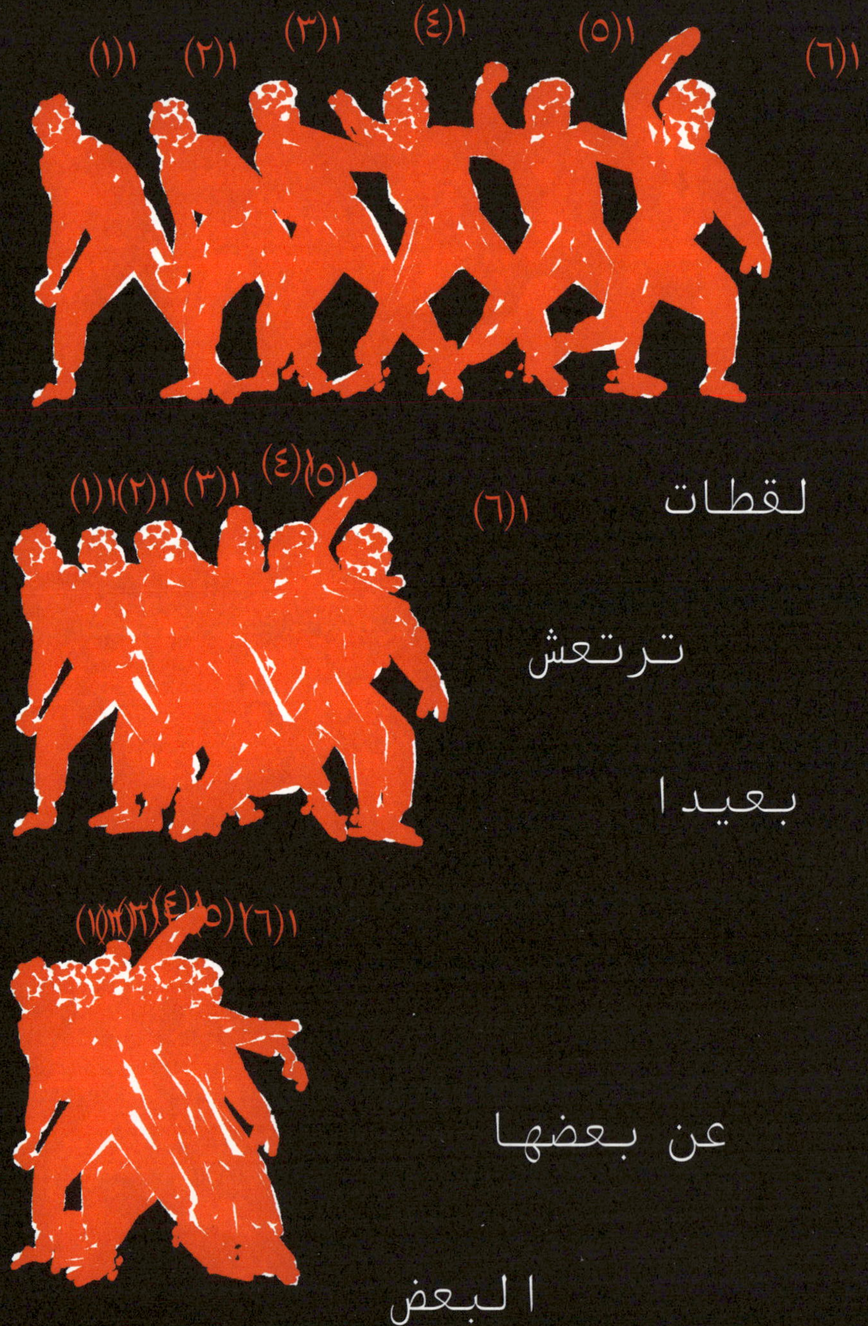

لقطات

ترتعش

بعيدا

عن بعضها

البعض

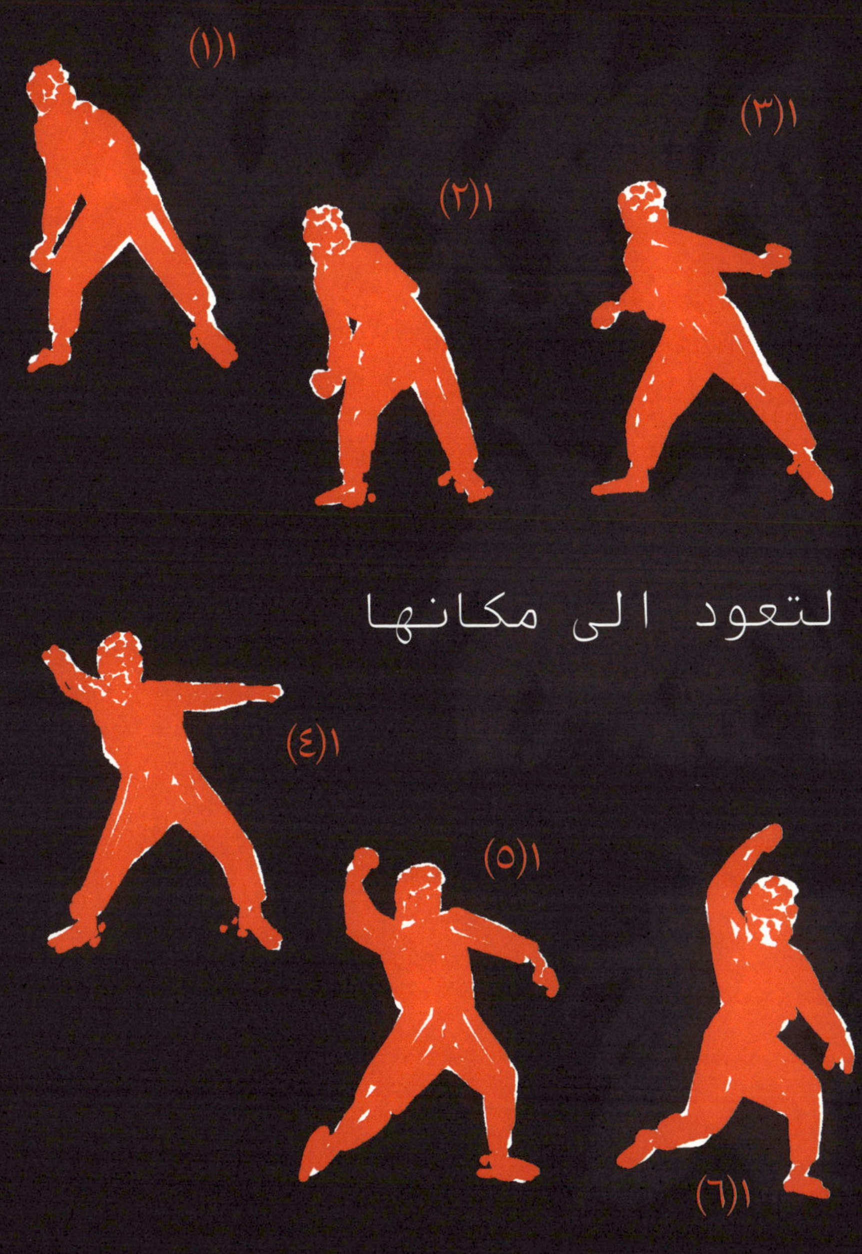

١(١)
١(٢)
١(٣)
لتعود الى مكانها
١(٤)
١(٥)
١(٦)

عبر الذكريات

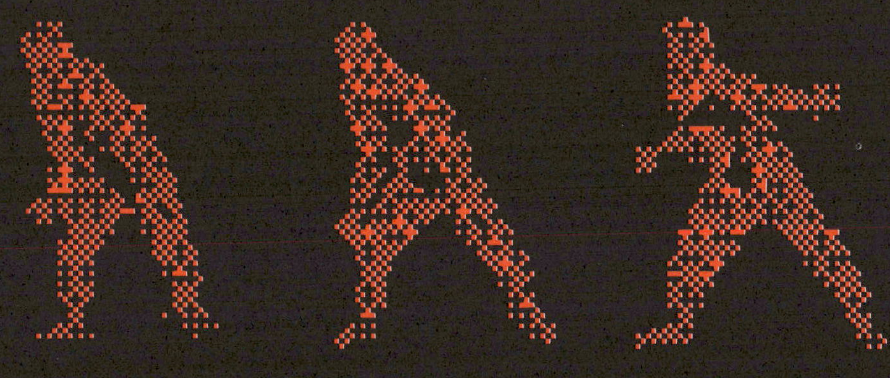

والشاشات

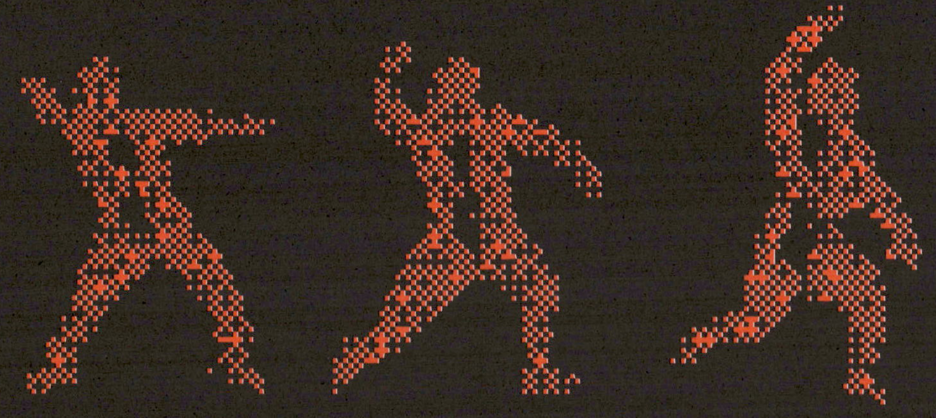

لتشهد "رمي"

عنجد؟

إن الصور في فلسطين لها منطق ثوري خاص بها. ومن بين الأشكال الاستثنائية لصناعة الصور التي تولّدت من النضال، هي صور الفلسطينيين في وقت اعتقالهم. ومن بين هذه الصور التاريخية الأيقونية صورة المناضلة والناشطة السياسية الفلسطينية الراحلة فاطمة البرناوي يوم الحكم عليها بالسجن المؤبد. وقد وقع الاعتقال في العاشر من تشرين الأول/أكتوبر، بعد بضعة أشهر من «نكسة عام ١٩٦٧». وقبل يومين من ذلك، في الثامن من تشرين الأول/أكتوبر، كان من المقرر أن تَعرِض «سينما صهيون» في القدس فيلمًا يحتفي بالحرب. وكانت فاطمة البرناوي تعيش في القدس في ذلك الوقت، وكانت منظِّمة سياسيًا مع «منظمة التحرير الفلسطينية». وفي ذلك اليوم، زرعت فاطمة، بمساعدة أختها إحسان، قنبلة في السينما احتجاجًا على عرض الفيلم واحتفالاته المتوالية. اعتُرِضَت العملية بعد وقت قصير من اكتشاف حارس أمن للقنبلة، التي سُرعان ما فككها مسؤولون إسرائيليون ولم تنفجر قط. تمكنت إحسان من الفرار إلى الأردن مباشرة بعد العملية، لكن فاطمة بقيت في القدس، حيث أُحتُجِزَت. بعد يومين، حكمت السلطات الإسرائيلية على فاطمة بالسجن مدى الحياة. وبينما كانت مكبلة، طلب منها القاضي الإسرائيلي أن تقف ساكنة لالتقاط صورة لها بُغية إعلان الخبر في الصحف العبرية. وفي تحدٍّ، أخرجت البرناوي لسانها، ساخرة من القاضي الإسرائيلي ومحكمته الزائفة والدولة الاستعمارية التي يمثلها.

لماذا قد تُخرِج مناضلة مثل فاطمة البرناوي لسانها بهذه الطريقة؟ ما الغرض من مثل هذه البادرة؟ ما نوع الصورة التي خلفتها البرناوي وراءها؟ في جلسات المحكمة، لم تُنكِر البرناوي مرة واحدة أي ادعاء ضدها، ولم تخلق صورة زائفة تنفي هويتها كشخصية منخرطة في الكفاح المسلح من أجل تحرير وطنها. ومع ذلك، كأيقونة للمقاومة الفلسطينية، فإن صورة فاطمة البرناوي لا تُشبه صور معاصريها. وبصرف النظر عن نوايا البرناوي أو دوافعها غير المقصودة، فقد تصرفت بناءً على رغبة في تقويض الصورة التي الْتُقطت لها في لحظة ضعف وهزيمة مفترضة. لم تُصوَّر قط وهي ترتدي ملابس عسكرية

أو تحمل كلاشينكوفًا أو أي سلاح آخر، كما هو الحال مع ليلى خالد على سبيل المثال. بدلًا من ذلك، قدَّمت صورة غير تقليدية للنضال من خلال ضعف موقعها نفسه وفقر التقنيات البصرية المتاحة لها في اللحظة التي أُعلن فيها عن سجنها. لقد قامت بجسدها وسلوكها المشاغب، وليس بالسلاح أو الرموز النضالية، بتخريب صورة كان من المفترض أن تُمثِّل لحظة هزيمة وأسر. من خلال توجيه نظرة ثاقبة الى الكاميرا، ومدّ لسانها الى الخارج، تحدَّت البرناوي الغرض من الصورة التي التقطها الإسرائيليون، وحولتها إلى صورة تظهر فيها كفلسطينية متحدية ومَرِحَة وحرة.

نشر المسؤولون الإسرائيليون صورة البرناوي في الصحف لإظهار القوة والظَفر الاستعماريين في القضاء على تهديد واحدة من السكان الأصليين. لكن الصورة اختُطِفَت بعد فترة وجيزة من قِبل الفلسطينيين الذين نشروها على نطاق واسع باعتبارها رمزًا للانتصار والصمود. وقد أدت عملية إعادة توظيف الصورة إلى زعزعة استقرار ظروفها المادية، واستخدامها كأداة لتعطيل ظروف صنعها، وكسر النظام الاستعماري للهيمنة والقمع الكامن في الصورة. الصورة المحددة في إطارها المستطيل ثُقِبَت بواسطة الموضوع الذي سعت إلى التقاطه، مما حولها من صورة أُنشئت بغرض المراقبة مع الأمل أن تصبح رمزًا للهزيمة، إلى صورة تشير إلى قوة المكبوتين.

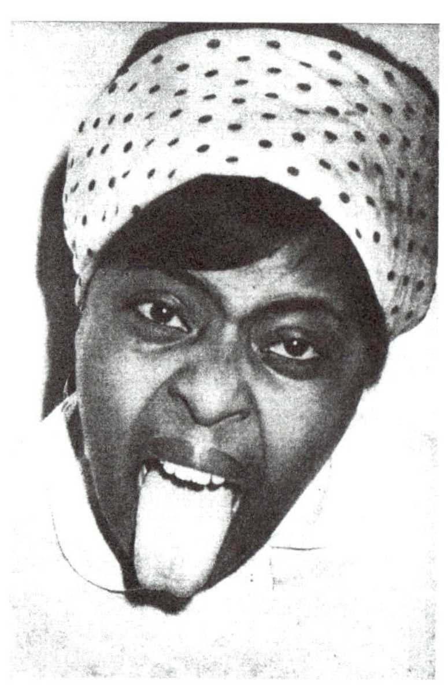

على الرغم من تفرُّد صورة البرناوي، فمن الممكن أن نربط بينها وبين سلالة أخرى من الصور التي أنتجها الفلسطينيون في وقت أسرهم. ويمكن فهم هذا الشكل من الإنتاج السلبي المتراكم للجماليات المقاوِمة أيضًا من خلال منطق الاختطاف. وكأن مثل هذه الممارسات الجماعية تُنظِّم تعطيلًا للمسار المحدد للتصوير الاستعماري القسري المشحون بالدافع إلى الهيمنة والمراقبة ونزع الصفة الإنسانية. وتؤدِّي هذه الاضطرابات إلى تضليل الصورة عن هدفها نحو هدف تحرري بديل، مما يخرّب عملية الالتقاط. ومن المهم تأطير جهود البرناوي ضعيفة التجهيز للتدخل في الصورة ضمن ممارسة مجتمعية تتجاوز الأيقنة والتبجيل لصورتها. ولتوضيح هذه الصلة، يجب أن نتجاوز قراءة بصرية تعمل حصريًا على المستوى التمثيلي، وننتقل إلى تحليل منهجي للاستراتيجيات الجمالية المستخدمة داخل التقليد الثوري الفلسطيني للاستيلاء على الصور الاستعمارية وإعادة تأهيلها إلى أدوات مناهضة للاستعمار. إن ما يجعل صورة البرناوي استثنائية هو ظروف إنتاجها ودوافع البرناوي الحدسية في لحظة الإخضاع. وكثيرًا ما تُلتَقَط صور مماثلة لفلسطينيين يبتسمون (وأحيانًا يرفعون علامة النصر إذا لم يكونوا مقيدين بالأصفاد) في لحظة الاعتقال. وما بدأ كبادرة حدسية خلال «الانتفاضة الأولى»، تطوَّر إلى تكتيك شائع مع «الانتفاضة الثانية». فالفلسطينيون من مختلف المناطق والأعمار، وعلى الرغم من إعادة تحديد الأراضي الفلسطينية من قِبل الاستعمار، كانوا يبتسمون للكاميرا في لحظة اعتقالهم وإخضاعهم لعنف الشرطة والجيش الإسرائيليين. يمكننا أن نرى ذلك، على سبيل المثال، عندما اعتُقل جاسر دويكات في الرابع من نيسان/أبريل ٢٠٢٢، ووجَّه جندي إسرائيلي بندقية إلى رأسه في زعترة، أو في حالة عدي مسودة الذي تعرض للهجوم وتم اقتياده إلى زنزانة سجن عند باب العامود في القدس في اليوم نفسه، أو محمد فاخوري في الأول من حزيران/يونيو ٢٠٢١، أو زينة الحلواني عندما كانت في مركز الشرطة قبل يومين من ذلك، أو روني شاهين ابن ترشيحا وهو يبتسم وقدم جندي تدوس رأسه أثناء احتجاجات عام ٢٠١٤ ضد مخطط برافر[٢٩].

تُعَد هذه الإيماءة البسيطة، التي تؤدّى كتكتيك بصري تخريبي، شكلًا فقيرًا ولكن ذو تأثير، من أشكال صُنع الصورة. تتسلَّل الإيماءات وتتدخَّل على مستوى التأليف (فمن يلتقط الصورة يتوقف عن امتلاك

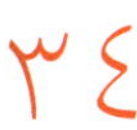

قوة سردها)، مما يؤدي إلى تغيير النموذج التمثيلي للفرد وسردية الحدث في لحظة الاعتقال على يد الإسرائيليين. غالبًا ما تؤدي هذه الإيماءات المتمثلة في الابتسام على الرغم من الأسر، إلى إشارة من نوع ما، وإرسال نداء إلى الرفاق والأقارب. إن الواقع الاستعماري الاستيطاني في العصر النيوليبرالي يجعل فعل التجمّع والتجمهُر أمرًا مستحيلًا، بل وغير قانوني في كثير من الأحيان. وبالنظر إلى هذه الظروف القمعية، فمن المذهل أن نلاحظ كيف تجد مثل هذه التكتيكات البصرية طريقها لتصبح جزءًا من معجم ولغة مناهضة الاستعمار المنتشرة في جميع أنحاء فلسطين. ويتأكّد ذلك بشكل خاص عندما نأخذ في الاعتبار كيف أنه لم تُعلِن أي قيادة قائمة رغبتها في اتباع هذه التكتيكات أو تكرارها، ولم يُتَفَق على هذه التكتيكات جماعيًا على أي مستوى من مستويات التنظيم السياسي، وإنما تم تقليدها بشكل حدسي وعفوي. فان هذه الممارسات تنص تقليد متمرّد مدمج في فلسفة جماليّة مُسيّسة، فلسفة ناشئة في الأزقة والشوارع كنظريّة مبتكرة من العاملات والعمال.

أصبح فعل الابتسام، واداء إيحاءات النصر بلغة الجسد، والتصرف برباطة جأش في لحظات الأسر والعنف أمرًا شائعًا للغاية الآن، حتى إن العديد من المعتقلين يُطلب منهم الابتسام عندما يلتقط أقاربهم صورًا لهم. وعندما يكون السجناء في جلسات الاستماع، يكون هناك دائمًا شخص ما في الغرفة مهمته تسريب صورة مختومة بابتسامة - كما لو كان يُهرِّب سجينًا إلى الخارج. تأتي هذه المطالبات والمحاولات من معرفة أن الصور ستنتشر على منصات التواصل الاجتماعي لمشاهدتها والتفاعل معها. هناك فهم عضوي لكيفية عمل اقتصادات الصور، وكيف تنتشر هذه الصور بدورها كإشارات. تقول الصورة المبتسمة: «لم نُهزَم بعد»، وهي تُلقِّن شكلًا من أشكال المرونة الجماعية لا تستطيع الآلة الإبادية الإسرائيلية تحديها[٣٠]. تنقل الصورة رغبة موضوعها إلى الآخرين للنهوض وأداء فعل مماثل، وبالتالي، يجب أن يكون تصنيعها وفقًا للمعايير المتَّبعة جماعيًا. الصورة نداء ينتظر استجابة، وهي تُطلِق صوتًا في بحثها عن صداها. وهذا النوع من الصور لا يعتمد على الشهود، بل يبحث عن مستمعين[٣١].

كما أن مجرد الابتسام يُعقِّد الأسئلة الأخلاقية المحيطة بتداول صور العنف. فالابتسامة تعيد توجيه النظرة من الطرف المكسور والعين الملطخة بالدماء والجذع المصاب إلى الوجوه الطيبة التي تُصرُّ على أن الصراع لا يبدأ ولا ينتهي داخل إطارات الصور التي تتَّخذ شكل أدلة. وبهذا تتزحزح الإساءة الاستعمارية ويُعاد توظيف الصورة لخدمة نضال سياسي بدلًا من تركها كحُطام استعماري. ومن خلال التركيز على الابتسامة بدلًا من تفاصيل أخرى لحَدَث المواجهة الاستعمارية، فإن هذا الشكل من صُنع الصورة يُخرِّب الصور الوثائقية المعتادة التي غالبًا ما تُفرِط في عرض لحظات العنف المشهدي الذي يُلحق بأجساد الفلسطينيين بُغية التعبئة من أجل القضية. وعلى الرغم من الإلحاحية التي نستهلك من خلالها هذا النوع من الصور وننشره، فمن الضروري إعادة النظر في العنف الذي تُعيد هذه الصور إنتاجه، خاصة بمجرد ربطها باقتصادات التداول الافتراضي. وفي كثير من الأحيان، تُغمَر الفضاءات الافتراضية بصور الموت والتشويه اللذين تفرضهما الصهيونية بشكل واضح على الحياة الفلسطينية. وكثيرًا ما يسعى الفلسطينيون أنفسهم، وحلفاؤهم، إلى توثيق الاحتلال وفضح حِدَّته الشنيعة، وهو ما قد يُشكِّل عملية مثمرة ضمن سجلات محددة. ومع ذلك، فإن التصوير المهيمن الذي أنتجته مثل هذه الممارسات الوثائقية يعيد إنتاج القمع المفروض، مما يؤدي في كثير من الأحيان إلى إضفاء طابع فيتيشي (شهواني) على الجسد الفلسطيني الجريح والمُعتدى عليه. كما تُسهِم مثل هذه الصور، سواء عمدًا أو بشكل سلبي، في مطالب السلطة بإثبات أن السلطة عنيفة وأن عنفها فعّال ومُجدي[٣٢].

٢٩
انظر/ي
Santiago Montag, "'Our Very Existence Here Is Our Resistance': Why Some Palestinians Smile When They Are Arrested by Israeli Soldiers." *Left Voice*, April 8, 2022. https://bit.ly/3AWtBWd.; Mahmoud Soliman, "Smiling as an Act of Resistance in Occupied Palestine." ROAR Magazine, August 11, 2021. https://bit.ly/4dVxHMT.

٣٠
انظر/ي
Alaa Abd el-Fattah, *You Have Not Yet Been Defeated: Selected Works 2011-2021.* (United States: Seven Stories Press, 2022).

٣١
انظر/ي
Fred Moten, "Black Mo'nin' in the Sound of the Photograph," in *In the Break: The Aesthetics of the Black Radical Tradition* (Minneapolis: University of Minnesota Press, 2003), 192-211.; Tina Campt, *Listening to Images* (Durham: Duke University Press, 2017), 3-45.

٣٢
Palestine Action. "Dismantling Israel's War Machine." Edited by Joud Al-Tamimi. *Weird Economies*, April 24, 2024. https://weird-economies.com/contributions/dismantling-israel-s-war-machine.

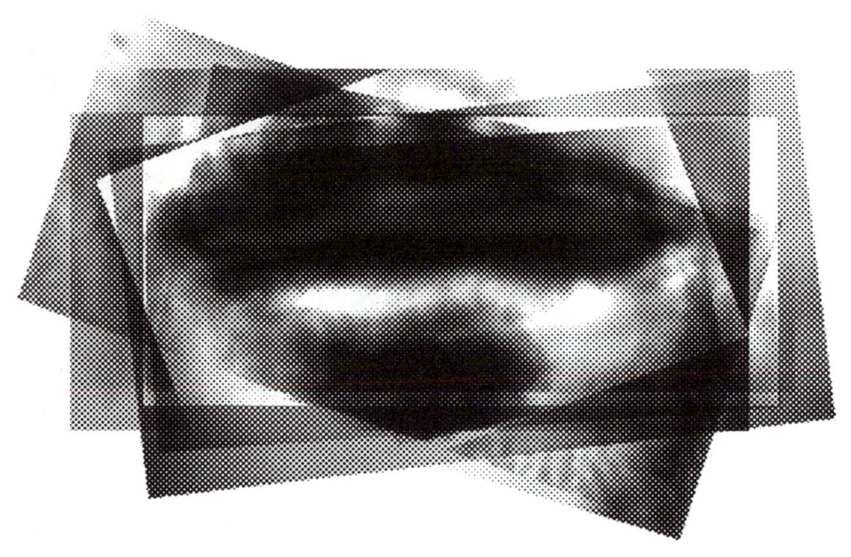

بعبـارة أخـرى، من خلال صُنـع ونشـر صـور الـعنف المشـهدي، نستسـلم للنظـام البصـري للسلطة السيـادية ومخططاتها الاقتصادية التي تُحـوِّل الصـور القـاسية إلى إعلانـات تـرّوج لكفاءة صناعة الأسلحة. التعـريض الزائـد - والإظهـار المُفـرط - للأجساد الفلسطينية التي أخضعتها القـوى الإستعمـارية علـى مـدى عقـود من الزمن، يأتي بمثـابة محـاولةٍ للتـركيز علـى حـالة فـردية لتمثّـل نظـام الإخضـاع والاستعمـار. وعندمـا يُطلَب من الأجسـاد المنتهَـكة أن تبتسـم في الصـورة، فإن ذلـك يجمِّـد لـحظة الاعتـداء الاستعمـاري في إطـار - ومن خلال استبعـاد الزمـان والمـكان الـلذين يتجـاوزان إطـار الصـورة، يتجـاوز الفلسـطينيون إعـادة إنتـاج الصـورة الـعنيفة وينتجـون بـدلًا من ذلـك إشـارة إلـى الصمـود من دون المسـاومة علـى الظـروف التي يعمـل فيها هذا الصمود أو التعتيـم عليها. نـحن جميعًـا نعلـم أن الفـرد المبتسـم في الصـورة، قـد تعـرض للانتهـاك وسـوف يتعـرض للانتهـاك، لـكن هذا لا يـعني أن هذا الانتهـاك يجب أن يُشيِّئـه أو يُسَـلِّعه أو يتاجـر بـه، ناهيـك عن الإفـراط في تمثيلـه إلـى الحـد الذي يُقلِّـل من حقيقة أن الفلسـطينيين ليسـوا مجـرد ضحايـا، بـل هـم مقاتلـون مُثابـرون يسـعون إلـى التحـرُّر.

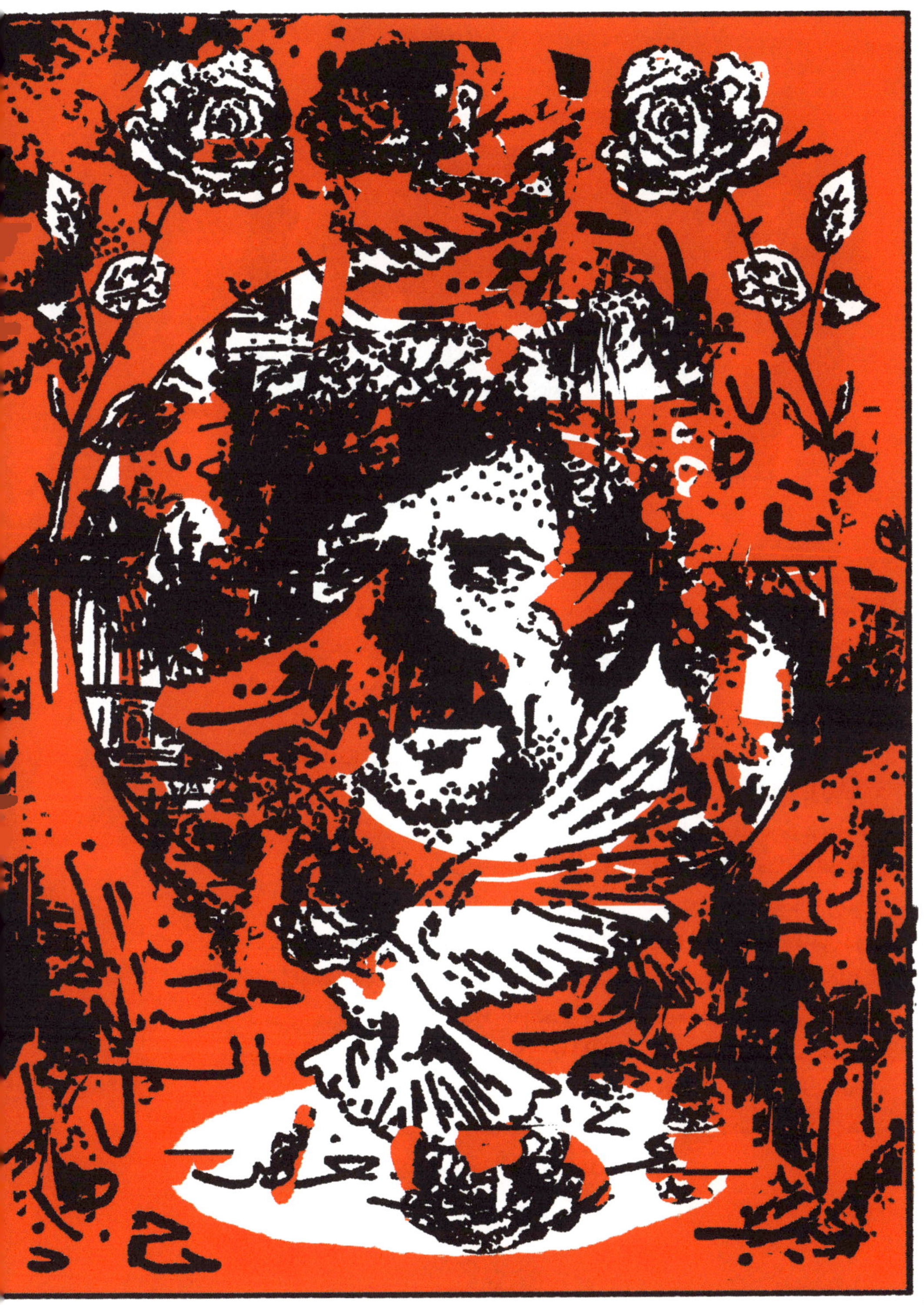

وينك

يمّا؟

غادرت صورتي منزلي وذهبت إلى الشوارع. لم تعد قادرة على تحمل الحبس. كانت بحاجة إلى الخروج. أمشي فأرى وجهي مرسومًا على الجدران. إنها صورة غريبة تلك التي اختاروها لي. أرى نفسي، ولكنني لم أعد ذلك الشخص. تُحدِّق الصورة فيَّ، وتُغرِّبني، مثل طفل يرى انعكاسه في المرآة للمرة الأولى، لكنها لا تتحرَّك عندما أتحرَّك. تظل ثابتة. أحيانًا، يغمرني وجودي على الطريق الرئيس، حيث وجهي مرسوم على العواميد والجدران الخرسانية، على صناديق الكهرباء الموضوعة خارج المنازل المهجورة، التي تتضاعف أحيانًا في صفوف وكأنها تحاول إخفاء شيء ورائها. وعندما أتجول في الأجزاء الأقل ارتيادًا من المدينة، أجد أحيانًا أجزاء مني في زوايا تبعث على الضحكة. بالأمس، على سبيل المثال، رأيت أنفي على الرصيف. بدا الأمر وكأن شخصًا ما لكَمَ أنفي، لكنني لم أشعر بأي شيء. وقبل أيام رأيت عيني، وعرفت أنها عيني لأنها تشبه عيني أمي. هذا ما كان يقوله أبي دائمًا: «عينيك مثل عينين إمك». يروق لي أن أرى أجزاء مني، كِسَرًا، قصاصات صغيرة. إنها أقرب إليَّ من صورة وجهي المُكبَّرة على لوحة إعلانية.

في الليل، يقولون إن الجو بارد بالخارج. غالبًا ما أجلس على الدرج بجوار الساحة مباشرة. أتذكر أنني رأيت شخصًا يُمزِّقني من على جدار كبير ويستخدمني كبطانية. الشريط الذي يربط ملصقات لوجهي بالحائط جعلها تبدو وكأنها منسوجات جدارية. بدا الأمر وكأن الملصقات نجحت في إبقائه دافئًا. اعتدت أن أكون في الشوارع كثيرًا، لكن الشوارع أصبحت غريبة علي. لم أتخيل قط أنه يمكن لهذه الساحة، التي أقضي فيها ليالي، أن تكون هادئة وسلمية إلى هذا

الحد. يقولون إنه بمجرد وصول صورتك إلى الشوارع فإنها تحل محلك. تصبحُ صورتَك، ثم تُمنع من الانضمام إلى الشوارع. حسنًا، ها أنا هنا، لكنني أشعر بالتشرُّد. يقول صديقي فيصل إن ذلك ربما يكون بسبب المطر[٣٣]. غسلني المطر من على الجدران إلى المجارير. قد يكون السبب أيضًا هو أن وجهي منتشر في جميع أنحاء المدينة، أو ربما تكسُّر وجهي هو الذي جعلني أشعر بما أشعر به. قد يكون السبب هو أنه في بعض أجزاء المدينة، بدأت صور جديدة تظهر وتغطي صوري. تبدو الوجوه الجديدة مألوفة في بعض الأحيان، لكنني لا أتعرف عليها في معظم الأحيان. لست متأكدًا من شعوري حيال الأمر. إنه لشيء مريح إلى حد ما ألا يكون وجهي في كل مكان. لأكون صريحًا، أشعر أحيانًا وكأن هناك الكثير مني لدرجة أنني لم أعد مرئيًا. أنا في كل مكان وبالتالي لستُ في أي مكان. قد يكون من الجيد أن يبدأ الآخرون في أخذ أدوارهم. هل هذا أناني؟ لا أتمنى هذا لأحد، لكن من الصعب المشي في المدينة عندما يكون الوجه الوحيد الذي تراه هو وجهك. عندما أرى وجوه الآخرين تظهر أشعر بالراحة. فهذا يؤكد لي أن الأمر مؤقَّت. من الجيد أن تكون بين آخرين يشاركونك تجربتك. عندما يختفي وجهي بين الحشود، يمنحني ذلك القدرة على إخفاء هويتي. يروق لي ذلك. يمدُّ أحدنا الرفقة للآخر ونختبئ في ظلال بعضنا البعض. إنه مجرد ثمن زهيد ندفعه قبل أن نختفي جميعًا معًا، في نهاية المطاف.

٣٣
فيصل دراج، بؤس الثقافة في المؤسسة الفلسطينية (بيروت، لبنان: دار الآداب، ١٩٩٦)، ٧-١٠.

٢

الأداء[2]

Performance

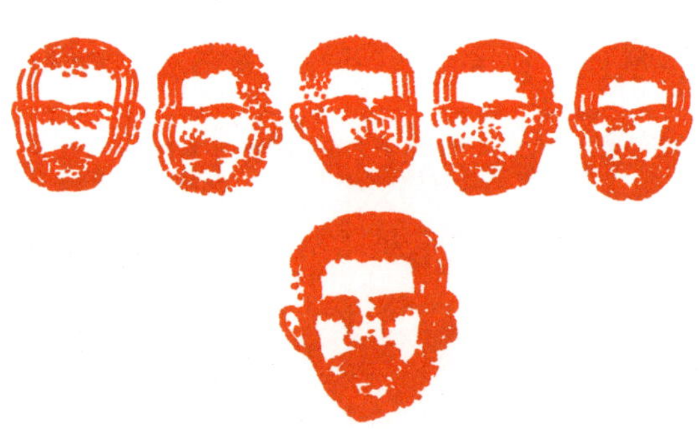

على راسي وعيني

في الثامن من تشرين الأول/أكتوبر ٢٠٢٢، وبينما كانت قوات الاحتلال الإسرائيلي تقوم بدوريات في مخيم شعفاط للاجئين في القدس، خرج عدي التميمي، أحد شباب المخيم، لخلق حَدَث من المواجهة الاستعمارية ردًا على مشاريع الاستيطان المتسارعة في القدس. قاد التميمي خلسةً سيارة مستأجرة عند نقطة تفتيش إسرائيلية تراقب أي شيء وأي شخص يدخل ويخرج من شعفاط، وأخرج مسدسًا مسروقًا وأطلق النار على الجنود من مسافة قريبة، مما أسفر عن مقتل أحدهم وإصابة آخَرين. ثم اختفى في الليل بينما أطلقت السلطات الإسرائيلية نداءً للبحث عنه، واصفةً إياه بأنه «رجل عربي أصلع يرتدي بدلة رياضية». وضعت قوات الاحتلال الإسرائيلي المخيم تحت الحصار للعثور على الشاب الأصلع الذي كانوا يبحثون عنه، وأجروا عمليات التفتيش الاستيطانية المعتادة في المنازل، وأوقفوا أي شخص يتطابق وصفه مع التميمي.

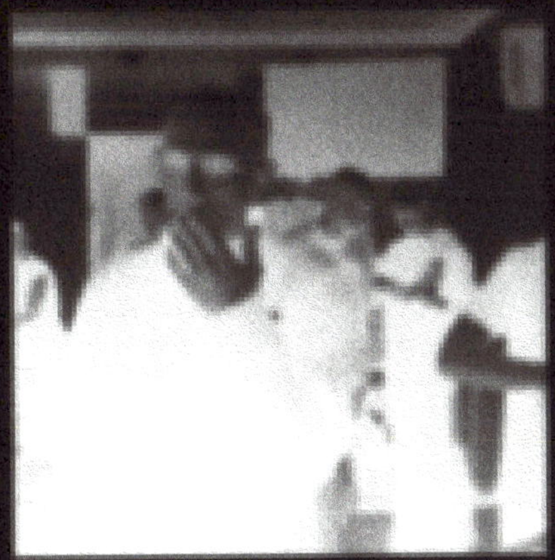

وفي شكل من أشكال الحماية أشبه بالمتاهة، قرّر لاجئو شعفاط الشباب تشتيت محاولات الجيش للعثور على التميمي. وباستخدام الأوصاف الاستعمارية وأساليب التنميط العرقي نفسها التي تستخدمها تكنولوجيا المراقبة الإسرائيلية للبحث عن التميمي، نجح سكان المخيم في خلق سراب. بدأ الإنترنت يتدفق ببطء بمقاطع فيديو وصور لرجال من شعفاط حلقوا رؤوسهم في المنازل وصالونات الحلاقة المحلية، وقد ارتدوا بدلًا رياضية من «أديداس» على طريقة التميمي. ثم تفرّقوا في شكل نُسَخ طبق الأصل منه في جميع أنحاء مخيم اللاجئين وشوارع القدس، مما جعل مهمة العثور عليه مستحيلة[٣٤]. لقد قامت مجموعة من الفلسطينيين بأداء ما فحصته آلة المراقبة الاستعمارية بالضبط من دون السماح لها بالوصول

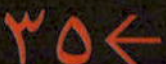

٣٥
طُردت قبائل بدو الجهالين وعرب السواحرة الفلسطينية من أراضيها في النقب أثناء نكبة عام ١٩٤٨، ثم مرة أخرى أثناء نكسة عام ١٩٦٧ وأُعيد توطينهم في خان الأحمر. وبعد اتفاقيات أوسلو، وخاصة في عامي ١٩٩٥ و١٩٩٧، أُخرجوا قسرًا من خان الأحمر للمرة الثالثة، ونقلوا عبر الحاويات إلى الضفة الغربية، وأخيرًا تفرقوا في المناطق المحيطة بنابلس وأريحا والخليل. وكما يقول الناشط عيد أبو غالية: «إن نكبة البدو مضاعفة. فنكبتهم الأولى هي إبعادهم القسري عن الأراضي التي يهيمون فيها، والثانية هي إجبارهم على الاستقرار في مكان واحد من دون حركة، والانفصال عن طريقة الحياة البدوية».

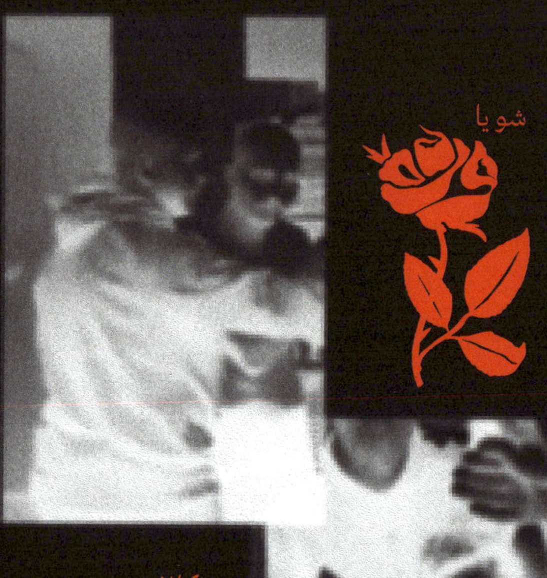

٣٤
«شباب فلسطينيون يحلقون رؤوسهم للتمويه على الاحتلال في بحثه عن منفذ عملية شعفاط». الجزيرة، ١٥ تشرين الأول/أكتوبر ٢٠٢٢.
https://bit.ly/3XnirS.

إلى *ما كانت تبحث عنه*. بنى الصُّلع في شوارع القدس درعًا واقيًا، ليس بالأسلحة وإنما بأجسادهم، لضمان سلامة التميمي من خلال محاكاة مظهره المُتصوَّر استعماريًا. كان الشعار الذي استخدموه في مناورتهم هو «برؤوسنا نحمي المقاومة»، مشرّعين شكلًا جديدًا من المقاومة، بينما نفّذوا حِيلة حطموا خلالها كاميرات الشوارع وأغلقوا الأزقة بالإطارات المشتعلة - منفذين لمنطق جدلي نضالي يدور حول الرؤية والتعتيم.

تمكّن مخيم صغير منزوع القوة ومُقطّع الأوصال من تأخير القبض على التميمي لمدة أسبوعين من خلال النضال الأدائي. وفي ليلة العشرين من تشرين الأول/أكتوبر ٢٠٢٢، كشف عدي التميمي عن نفسه طواعية، حاملًا جسده إلى نهايته المتوقعة من خلال مواجهة الجنود الصهاينة بمسدس، بمفرده، من دون حماية أو نية للهروب. تمكّن

من التسلُّل إلى مستوطنة معاليه أدوميم، التي بنيت على أنقاض قرية الخان الأحمر، واطلق النار على الجنود الذين كانوا يحرسون المستوطنة[٣٥]. أُطلقت النيران عليه عدة مرات واخترق الفولاذ الاستعماري جسده، مما تسبب في انهياره على الأرض. حبس التميمي أنفاسه الأخيرة، واستمر في إطلاق النار باتجاه الجنود حتى فاقَ الدمُ نيرانه. كان التميمي واحدًا من الكثيرين الذين قدموا تضحيات فردية لتحدي المحاولات الإسرائيلية لتصفية المقاومة الفلسطينية لصالح مشروعها الاستعماري. لكن ليس كل موت هو موت يحمله كثيرون. يموت العديد من المقاتلين في عزلة، وأحيانًا في الحبس الانفرادي بعد أعوام من السجن، ويموت آخرون تحت أنقاض الركام التي تستمر جاثمة على الرغم من تفسُّخ أجسادهم. تقيس آلة الموت الصهيونية خوارزميًا المسافة بيننا، والقدرات النفسية التي تُحدِّد دوافعنا، والروابط الاجتماعية الجريحة التي على وشك التمزُّق، وذلك بُغية حساب حركات رقص الاستعمار الذي يسعى إلى عزلنا وتفتيتنا وتدميرنا. إن شعار «برؤوسنا نحمي المقاومة» يعني رفض الاستسلام لمثل هذه الحركات المميتة، هذه الرقصة الفتّاكة. بدلًا من ذلك، أنتج شباب شعفاط لغة مُجسَّدة للمقاومة ورفقة النضال من السلبي[٣٦]. ومن خلال الجماليات، تتشكّل التجمُّعات النضالية، وتُختَرَع اللغات والمعرفة غير القابلة للقياس، وتظهر الاندماجات الاجتماعية على الرغم من كل محاولات حَتّها.

وباستخدام هذه المناورات، يفشل النموذج الاستعماري الاستيطاني الثابت، وتنعكس الأدوار. وتُتَحدّى وتُرفَض باستمرار العلاقة بين كاميرات المراقبة وعيون المحتلين، وأجساد الفلسطينيين التي تخضع للفحص والتدقيق. ويتوقف شباب شعفاط عن الوجود كأهداف للمراقبة، ويصبحون مؤدِّين نَشِطين يُوظِّفون أجسادهم الخاضعة للمراقبة بوعي. وفي الوقت نفسه، يعاد تعريف المحتلين كجمهور يجلس على حافة أبراج المراقبة الخاصة مع خطر السقوط الوشيك. أعينهم مُقتلعة، وشاشاتهم عبارة عن مسرح. لم يخرج شباب شعفاط من النظام البصري الاستعماري، بل نحتوا مساحة سلبية داخله. استخدموا الادوات الجمالية المتاحة لهم - أجسادهم - لخلق توترات وانقطاعات وصدوع بين المفاهيم المفترضة للظهور والظهور المفرط والاختفاء والشفافيَة والمحاكاة.

تكرار التمعّن في هذه الاحداث يدفعنا للشعور بالذهول والانعاش والدهشة، إزاء إبداع روح جماعية ترفض الإنكسار في ظل هذه الظروف القمعية. لكن ما يدفع الكثيرين منا إلى تجسيد وأداء هذه الممارسات الجمالية الثورية والتي هي بالغة الخطورة في جوهرها، بسبب إفقار شكلها، والردود القاتلة الناتجة بسبب ممارستها، هو حقيقة مفادها أنه ليس لدينا ما نخسره، وأن الديون التي تراكمت علينا (التي ندين بها والتي نستحقها) لن تُسدَّد أبدًا ما لم نلغيها وبأنفسنا[٣٧]. إن هذه الأشكال الجمالية للمقاومة السياسية تُشكّل ضرورةً للحفاظ على الوجود في ظل كيان استعماري استيطاني ساحق يعمل باستمرار على القضاء على الحضور الفلسطيني على الأرض، وكسر الروح الفلسطينية بالكامل حتى تُطرح المقاومة وتُنزع وتُصفّى من المعادلة. بعد ثلاثة أشهر من استشهاد عدي التميمي، في الخامس والعشرين من كانون الثاني/ يناير ٢٠٢٣، اقتحم أكثر من ثلاثمائة جندي إسرائيلي مخيم شعفاط للاجئين في عملية لهدم منزل عائلة عدي التميمي[٣٨]. حاول شباب ورجال المخيم تشكيل حاجز بأجسادهم يحيط بمنزل المقاتل الراحل، لكن الانتقام كان وحشيًا. تعرّض العديد من الفلسطينيين للضرب المبرّح والتشويه اللذين تركا على أجسادهم علامات جروح الرصاص وكدمات الهراوات، بينما رمى آخرون الحجارة على الجنود من بعيد. أحد سكان المخيم، محمد علي محمد علي، الذي كان في السابعة عشرة من عمره، أصيب برصاصة، وعلى الرغم من نقله إلى المستشفى، فإن جسده لم يستطع التغلّب على الجروح التي أصيب بها. وعند الغسق، أعلن استشهاده، وأُعلِنَ منزل التميمي أطلالًا[٣٩].

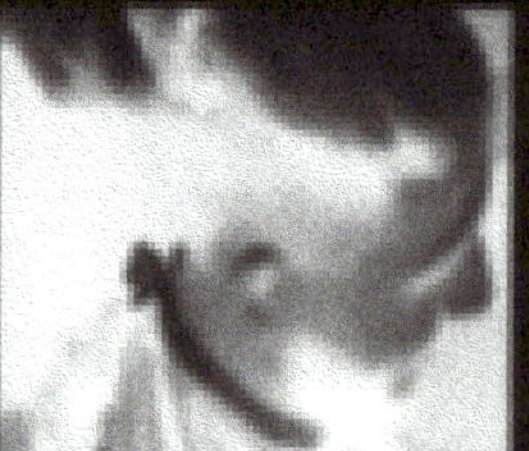

٣٦
Basel Abbas and Ruanne Abou-Rahme, *May amnesia never kiss us on the mouth*, 2021–, https://mayamnesia.com.

٣٧
Denise Ferreira Da Silva, *Unpayable Debt*. (Germany: MIT Press, 2022).

٣٨
كل التفاصيل المتعلقة بوفاة التميمي، إلى جانب وصف تصرُّفاته وإجراءات هدم منزله، يمكن العثور عليها في صحف صهيونية مثل «يسرائيل هايوم» و«واينت» وغيرهما، والتي أرفض إدراج روابطها هنا بسبب خطابها العنصري والاستعماري واللاإنساني.

٣٩
المصدر نفسه.

أنا شبح، أنا الآخر

تُذكّرنا هذه الإيماءات التمثيلية المجسَّدة بالاستراتيجيات التي استخدمتها النساء الفلسطينيات خلال «الثورة العربية الكبرى» ١٩٣٦-١٩٣٩. في ذلك الوقت، أضرب العمال، وأوقفوا عملهم لدى السلطات الاستعمارية البريطانية في جميع أنحاء البلاد. حمل المزارعون السلاح وبدلًا من فلاحة أراضيهم أصبحوا مقاتلين مُلتحمين بالأرض، يحمونها من المستوطنات، والأرض بدورها تحميهم. نشأت طبقة فتّاكة من الثوار لمعارضة واقتلاع الحكم الاستعماري البريطاني لفلسطين الذي كان ميسّرًا للاستيطان الصهيوني المتسارع. وعلى الرغم من أن السرديات الاستعمارية للحَدَث حاولت تأطيره باعتباره أعمال شغب إجرامية مبعثرة، فإنه يظل من بين الاحتجاجات والاضرابات المنظَّمة المناهضة للاستعمار الأكثر تكلفة للامبراطورية البريطانية خلال القرن العشرين[٤٠]. والأمر اللافت للنظر في هذا الحَدَث التاريخي، لأغراضنا هنا، هو التكتيكات النضالية الأدائية والصوتية والبصرية المستخدمة لمواجهة الإدارة الاستعمارية. كان لهذه التكتيكات علاقة بالديناميكيات الاجتماعية الجندرية السائدة داخل المجتمع الفلسطيني والطرق التي كانت تُصوّر بها هذه الديناميكيات، وتَشكّلت بها وفقًا لذلك، من قِبل حكومة الانتداب وحلفائها الصهاينة.

(ن)

(غ)

٤٠
Matthew Kelly, *The Crime of Nationalism: Britain, Palestine, and Nation-Building on the Fringe of Empire.* (United States, University of California Press, 2017).

خلال الأعوام التي سبقت الثورة، كان لكل طبقة اجتماعية وسياسية، اعتمادًا على جغرافيتها ومساكنها، الملابس التي تدل على وضعها/ مكانتها. ارتدى الرجال الحضريون الحديثون بدلات مُفصَّلَة، في حين ارتدت النساء الحضريات قمصانًا وتنانير بأزرار. وارتدى القوميون العرب المتمدنون الطربوش، في حين امتنع عن ارتدائه رجال الأعمال الذين فضلوا العمل مع الإنكليز. وارتدى المزارعون جلابيب خفيفة طويلة لحمايتهم من التعرض لأشعة الشمس أثناء العمل في الأرض لساعات طويلة، ولإبقاء أجسامهم مُعرَّضة للهواء. وغالبًا ما ارتدى الرجال ***الحطة*** و***العقال*** - غطاء الرأس التقليدي لمختلف مجتمعات المنطقة المصنوع من قماش خفيف (الحطة)، والذي يثبَّت بحبل مزدوج مصنوع من شعر الماعز لإبقاء القماش ملتصقًا بالرأس (العقال). في حين ارتدت النساء ***الطرحة***، وهي قطعة قماش خفيفة تغطي الرأس والكتفين، وتُثبَّت بالرأس عن طريق لفها على الشعر. وقد تجسدت كل هذه الدلالات في ألبسة مختلفة حملت معها معان اجتماعية وسياسية سواء داخل المجتمع الفلسطيني أو في الطريقة التي نظرت بها إليها حكومة الانتداب وموظفوها. وبينما ظلت هذه الدلالات علامات على الاختلاف الطبقي والارتباط السياسي، فقد استُخدمت كأسلحة لتوصيل معان بديلة خلال ثورة ١٩٣.

(ف)

هناك مطلب مُعيَّن رفعه القوميون الفلسطينيون خلال أعوام الثورة يُطرَح في كثير من الأحيان لانتقاد ذكورية النضال الوطني الفلسطيني. خاطب هذا المطلب النساء، وشجَّعهم على الشروع في ارتداء الحجاب، عبر مختلف الخطوط الاجتماعية والسياسية والحضرية والطبقية الطرفية. وعلى الرغم من أن النظام الاجتماعي الأبوي في فلسطين لا يزال منتشرًا بلا شك، فإن هذا المطلب التاريخي الخاص كان يحمل دوافع إضافية. لا يعني هذا تجاهل التنظيم الاجتماعي الأبوي، ولا ترتيب ظروف العنف على أساس هرمي، أو إعطاء الأولوية لبعض موضوعات العنف على غيرها، ليتم بعدها إجراء تقييمات حول البُنَى التي تتطلب المزيد من الإلحاح. ولكنه يعني صياغة

(س)

تحليل للذاتيات السياسية وغير المسيسة، والطرق التي تقاوم بها هذه الذاتيات، على الرغم من تورطها في بنى متشابكة من القمع. إن المنطق الذي يقوم عليه توقُّع ارتداء الحجاب من النساء صِيغَ كاستراتيجية نضالية لإرباك العدو الاستعماري، مع الحفاظ على عمليات إعادة الهيكلة الأبوية القومية في المجتمع الفلسطيني، وقد فهمت النساء الفلسطينيات هذا النموذج ووجّهنه نحو غاياتهن السياسية الذاتية.

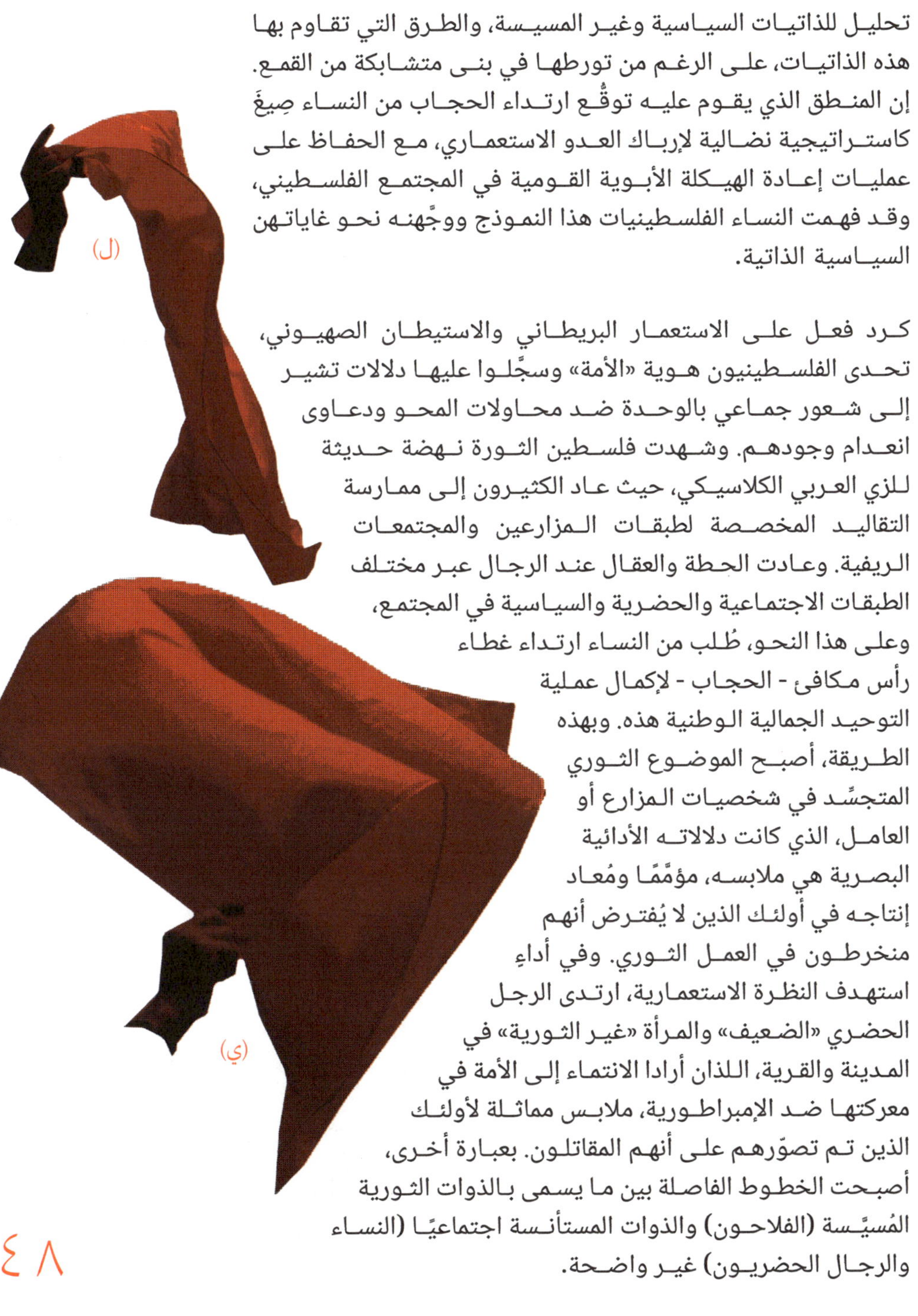

كرد فعل على الاستعمار البريطاني والاستيطان الصهيوني، تحدى الفلسطينيون هوية «الأمة» وسجّلوا عليها دلالات تشير إلى شعور جماعي بالوحدة ضد محاولات المحو ودعاوى انعدام وجودهم. وشهدت فلسطين الثورة نهضة حديثة للزي العربي الكلاسيكي، حيث عاد الكثيرون إلى ممارسة التقاليد المخصصة لطبقات المزارعين والمجتمعات الريفية. وعادت الحطة والعقال عند الرجال عبر مختلف الطبقات الاجتماعية والحضرية والسياسية في المجتمع، وعلى هذا النحو، طُلب من النساء ارتداء غطاء رأس مكافئ - الحجاب - لإكمال عملية التوحيد الجمالية الوطنية هذه. وبهذه الطريقة، أصبح الموضوع الثوري المتجسِّد في شخصيات المزارع أو العامل، الذي كانت دلالاته الأدائية البصرية هي ملابسه، مؤمَّمًا ومُعاد إنتاجه في أولئك الذين لا يُفترض أنهم منخرطون في العمل الثوري. وفي أداءٍ استهدف النظرة الاستعمارية، ارتدى الرجل الحضري «الضعيف» والمرأة «غير الثورية» في المدينة والقرية، اللذان أرادا الانتماء إلى الأمة في معركتها ضد الإمبراطورية، ملابس مماثلة لأولئك الذين تم تصوّرهم على أنهم المقاتلون. بعبارة أخرى، أصبحت الخطوط الفاصلة بين ما يسمى بالذوات الثورية المُسيَّسة (الفلاحون) والذوات المستأنسة اجتماعيًا (النساء والرجال الحضريون) غير واضحة.

(ح)

وكان لهذا التوحيد قيمة نضالية تتجاوز قيمته الرمزية. فقبل الثورة، كان التحالف البريطاني-الصهيوني يراقب باستمرار الفلسطينيين الذين يعبرون الأراضي البرية من أبراج المراقبة والمواقع العسكرية، ويميز بين أوضاعهم الاجتماعية عن طريق هيئتهم وملابسهم. وهذا يعني أن غطاء الرأس ميَّزَ تلقائيًا المزارعين والمزارعات عن غيرهم، وميَّزت البدلة رجال الأعمال عن المناضلين والرجال عن النساء. لكن بعد العودة إلى العادات الكلاسيكية، أصبح من الصعب على البريطانيين وأزلامهم التمييز بين أولئك الذين يعبرون الأراضي لنقل الأسلحة، وأولئك الذين يسافرون لشراء أو بيع المحاصيل، والمتجولين بلا هدف. إن ما أصبح مثيرًا للاهتمام مع تطور هذه العروض الأدائية، لم يكن كيف استغل الرجالُ النساءَ في مشاريعهم المناهضة للاستعمار، بل كيف استغلت النساءُ النظامَ الاجتماعي الاستعماري الذي أُنتِجَت فيه النساء كذوات منزلية، لترسيخ أنفسهن في النضال من أجل الاستقلال السياسي وتحرير أنفسهن وأرضهن.

وتشهد الروايات الشفوية والذاكرة الجماعية على أن العديد من النساء أدّين ما بدا إسقاطًا جنسيًا استعماريًا لحياتهن المنزلية المستعمرة، بينما كن في الواقع مندمجات تمامًا في النضال من أجل تحرير فلسطين من دون الحاجة إلى حمل السلاح أو أداء خيال محدود لما يُشكِّل نضالًا مناهضًا للاستعمار[٤١]. ويتضح هذا البُعد السياسي الذي نُفِّذ من خلال المجال الاجتماعي بشكل واضح في فيلم «ليلى والذئاب» (١٩٨٤) للمخرجة هايني سرور، حيث يُنظَر إلى النساء الفلسطينيات، على مدار الأحداث التاريخية، على أنهن منخرطات بنشاط في النضال من أجل التحرير. إن مشاركة النساء، كما تراها سرور، لا تتجسَّد من خلال حملهن الواضح للكلاشينكوف أو غيره من الأسلحة، بل من خلال أدائهن الذي تبدو عليه عاديّة العمل المنزلي: حمل كميات كبيرة من الطعام والمحاصيل من مكان إلى آخر، والغناء والرقص في مناسبات اجتماعية مثل حفلات الزفاف، وإقامة مراسم تقليدية أخرى محصورة في المجال الاجتماعي ومحظورة من المجال السياسي. ومع ذلك، يكشف لنا الفيلم عن هذه الأنشطة باعتبارها سياسية بطبيعتها، لأن الأسلحة والذخيرة كانت مخبأة

داخل سلال القمح التي حملتها النساء على رؤوسهن. وتحت أصوات الغناء والرقص الاحتفالية، كانت المجالس الجماعية تُعقَد للتخطيط للهجوم التالي على الأعداء المستعمِرين. وتبيّن أن الشَّبكة الذهبية للعروس كانت تُستخدم كشكل من أشكال نقل الموارد من منطقة إلى أخرى. هذا التعقيد في الأدوار والأبعاد الاجتماعية يُتاح لنا بمجرد أن ندرك أداء النساء فيما يتعلق بحياتهن المنزلية المؤنثة من خلال طلاقتهن الجمالية في توظيف مثل هذه الاستراتيجيات سياسيًا. لم تكن النساء الفلسطينيات واعيات فقط بالظروف الأبوية التي حَدَّدت أدوارهن الاجتماعية، بل كن واعيات أيضًا بنظرة العدو الاستعماري إليهن باعتبارهن نساء مستعمَرات. لقد أدين حيواتهن المنزلية المستعمَرة للمستعمرين الصهاينة والبريطانيين، بينما اختطفن أيضًا النظام الاجتماعي الأبوي الذي عشن في ظله بين الرجال عمومًا.

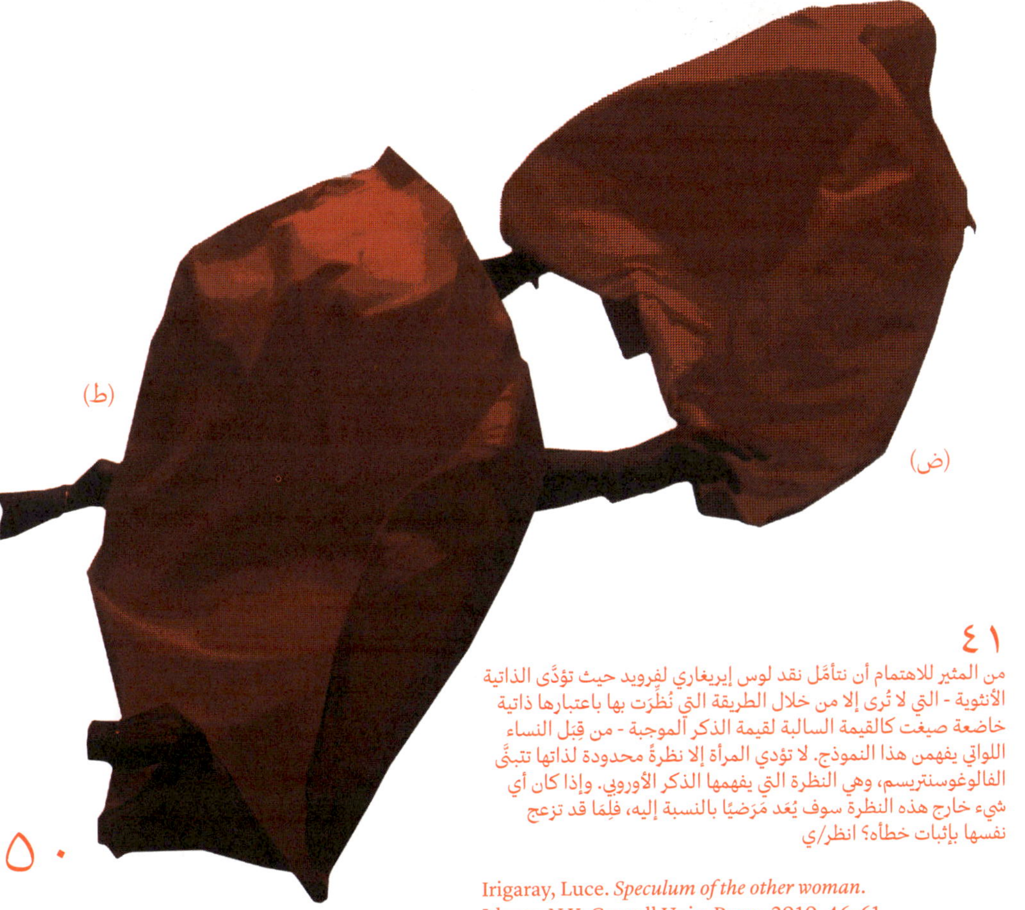

(ط)

(ض)

٤١
من المثير للاهتمام أن نتأمَّل نقد لوس إيريغاري لفرويد حيث تؤدَّى الذاتية الأنثوية - التي لا تُرى إلا من خلال الطريقة التي نُظِرَت بها باعتبارها ذاتية خاضعة صيغت كالقيمة السالبة لقيمة الذكر الموجبة - من قِبَل النساء اللواتي يفهمن هذا النموذج. لا تؤدي المرأة إلا نظرةً محدودة لذاتها تتبنَّى الفالوغوسنتريسم، وهي النظرة التي يفهمها الذكر الأوروبي. وإذا كان أي شيء خارج هذه النظرة سوف يُعَد مَرَضيًا بالنسبة إليه، فلِمَا قد تزعج نفسها بإثبات خطأه؟ انظر/ي

Irigaray, Luce. *Speculum of the other woman.* Ithaca, N.Y: Cornell Univ. Press, 2010. 46-61.

A Choreography of

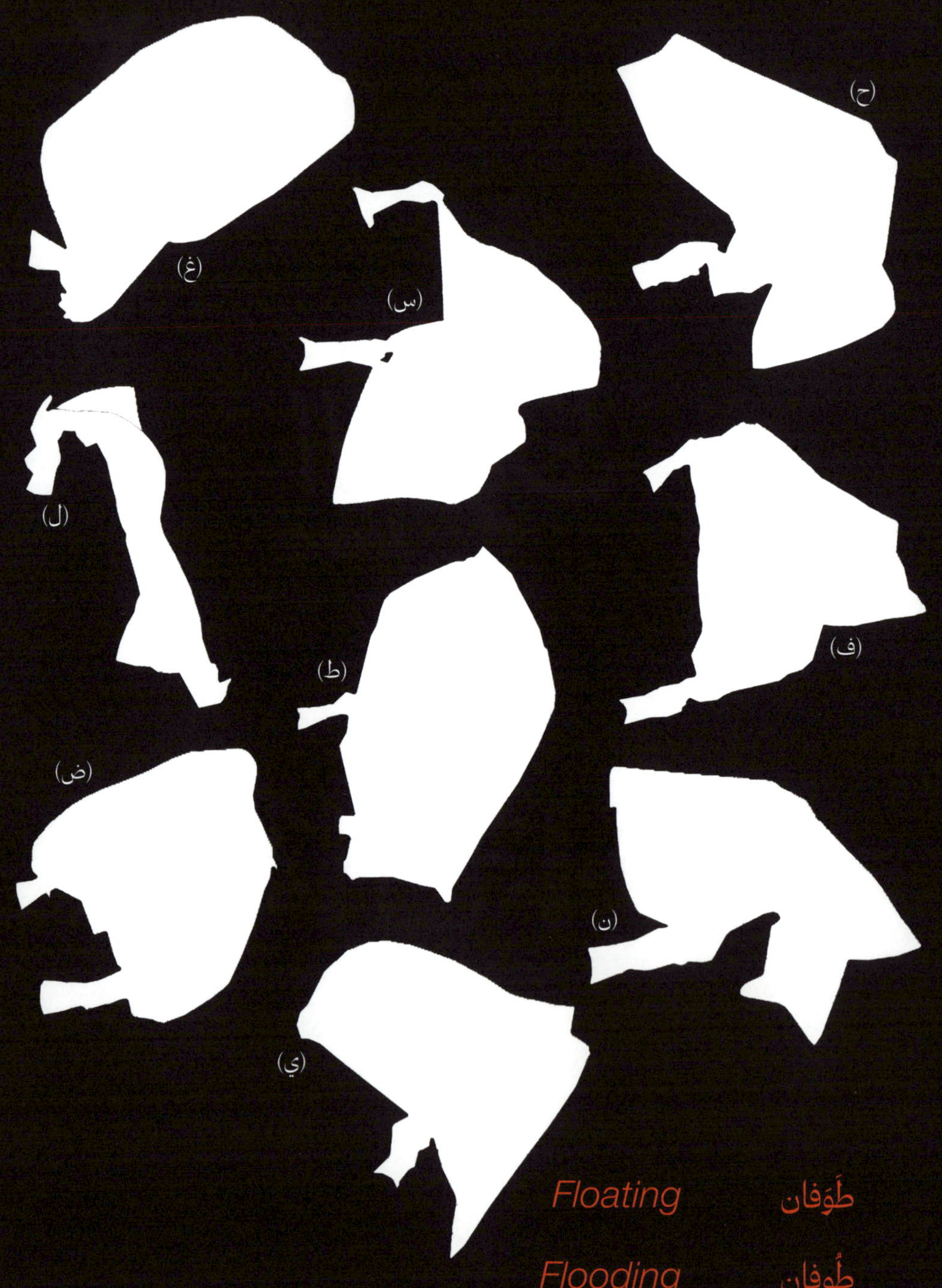

Floating طَوفان

Flooding طُوفان

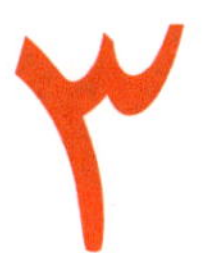

الصوت[3]

Sound

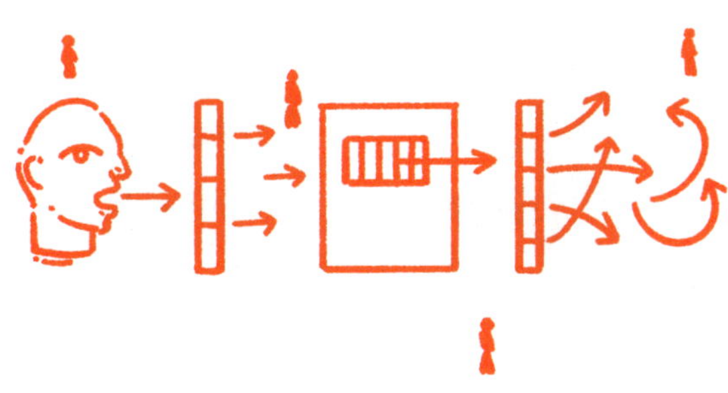

إن أصداء مثل هذه الاستراتيجيات الجمالية التي تطورت خلال أعوام الثورة، سواء كانت أدائية أو صوتية أو غير ذلك، تتردد حتى يومنا هذا. في كتابته عن «الثورة العربية الكبرى» عام ١٩٣٦، التي أطلقت عليها وحدة الاستخبارات الاستعمارية الصهيونية «الهاغاناه» اسم «الأحداث» - والتي عارضت في الوقت نفسه الانتداب البريطاني، والاستغلال الرأسمالي للمزارعين الذين لا يملكون أرضًا، وتصاعد العلاقات الطبقية العرقية، والاستيطان الصهيوني في فلسطين - يدرس ماثيو كيلي الإطار التجريمي للانتداب البريطاني باعتباره أداة ثورية مضادة لنزع الطابع السياسي[٤٢]. فالمجال الذي يسميه «السياسي الإجرامي» في حالة الانتداب، والذي عمل على أُسس خطابية وقانونية، استخدم فئة المجرم كمرادفة لفئة القومي العربي، فأضفى طابعًا رسميًا تجريميًا على التنظيم السياسي المناهض للاستعمار والرأسمالية. وليس من قبيل المصادفة أن يكتمل «قانون ١٩٣٦» ويدخل حيز التنفيذ في أيلول/سبتمبر من ذلك العام، أي بعد خمسة أشهر من اندلاع الثورة، حيث استُخدم كأساس متين حاول من خلاله التشريع القانوني الاستعماري الإطاحة بما هدّد صلاحيته[٤٣]. وهكذا أنتجت «الثورة العربية الكبرى» في الفترة ١٩٣٦-١٩٣٩ أكبر عدد من الفلسطينيين المعتقلين في ظل حكومة الانتداب، ولكنها أنتجت أيضًا تقليدًا جماليًا ناشئًا للثورة - اختراع شكل جديد للتنظيم السياسي.

خلافًا للصور التي يسهل تحويلها إلى سلعة، والتي تُلتَقَط في إطار، وتُغلَق، وتُجمَّد في الزمن، وتُميَّز بالقيمة، وتُنزع ملكيتها أثناء تداولها، فإن الصوت والموسيقى لاماديين، وعابرين، وثاقِبين، ومُتحرِّكين. فالصوت يسافر، ويتسرَّب، وينزلق، وينزف. وإذا كان مرتفعًا فإنه يسبب الضرر، وإذا كان منخفضًا، أو مكتومًا، أو مُخفَّتًا، أو صامتًا فإنه يزعزع

٤٢
Matthew Kelly, *The Crime of Nationalism.*

٤٣
Matthew Hughes “The banality of brutality: British Armed forces and the repression of the Arab revolt in Palestine, 1936-39’.” *The English Historical Review*,124 (507) (2009): 313 - 354.

الاستقرار، وفي أحيان أخرى يهرب. لقد طَوَّرت النساء الفلسطينيات نوعًا من الأغاني المشفَّرة بِبُنَى غنائية ولحنية وتأليفية تُخفي رسائل سياسية موجهة إلى السجناء وتُعرَف باسم «المشفَّرات». والمنطق الكامن وراء المشفَّرات هو أنها تنبثق عن تقاليد الغناء الفلكلوري الفلسطيني القائمة، والتي تستحضر في كثير من الأحيان الواقع المعاش المباشر لفلسطين. من أغاني الاستسقاء التي تستدعي المطر في مواسم الجفاف، إلى تلك التي تدعم الحياة وتتكلم عن الأرض وإليها، إلى الأغاني التي تدور عن المزارعين والتجار الذين يسافرون بعيدًا والمصحوبة بدعوات من أجل عودتهم سالمين، وغيرها من الأغاني التي تدور حول الصعوبات والتحديات التي يفرضها الاستيلاء على الأراضي ونزع الملكية والنضال من أجل السيادة. لكن المشفَّرات ليست مجرد أغانٍ. فمن خلال شكلها المضلِّل باعتبارها فولكلورية وغير ذات أهمية، انتشرت بشكل تلقائي، واستبطنَت الرسائل السياسية داخل شكلها الجذَّاب بشكل مُخادِع، بحثًا عن أولئك المجهَّزين للاستماع إليها. وهذا هو السبب في أن المشفَّرات رائجة واستثنائية في الوقت نفسه. بمعنى ما، تشبه هذه الأغاني أغان أخرى وتستحضر ألحانًا أخرى. ومن المرجح أن تُغنى في سياقات مختلفة، مثل مواسم الحصاد أو حفلات الزفاف. وعندما تذهب النساء الفلسطينيات لزيارة السجون البريطانية والصهيونية لرؤية أحبائهن ورفاقهن الأسرى، فلن يكون من الغريب أن يغنين المشفَّرات في الخارج أثناء الانتظار، أو أثناء الزيارة. فهن يغنين أغانيهن هناك كما يفعلن ذلك في أي مكان آخر.

والأغنية الأكثر إتيانًا على الذكر لهذا النوع الغنائي في وقتنا هذا، والتي تحظى بشعبية والمعروفة لدى العديد من الفلسطينيين بسبب انتشارها كأغنية شعبية بين العديد من الموسيقيين التجاريين، هي «يا طالعين الجبل». جذور هذه الأغنية راسخة في التربة الحارة لثورة ١٩٣٦. فمع تحول المقاتلين إلى أسرى، سارت نساء الثورة نحو السجون للغناء لهم.

تنتمي الأغنية إلى سلالة معينة من المشفَّرات، والتي تستخدم جميعها منطق التشفير نفسه، المعروف باسم «المُلالاة». «يا طالعين الجبل»، مثل غيرها من «المُلالات»، شُفِّرت باستخدام نظامين تقنيين. الأول يكمن في طريقة غنائها: تتكشف كلمات الأغنية بشكل غير مفهوم للآذان التي لا تألفها بسبب إضافة مقاطع لفظية زائدة بحرف «ل»

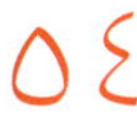

متبوع بحرف علة بين الحروف والكلمات، مما يكسف الكلمات بصوت متكرر. وتُحجَب الكلمات المنطوقة باستخدام الزغاريد والحشو اللفظي المتكرر. في الممارسة العملية، تبدأ الكلمات بـ«يا طالعين عين للل الجبل يا موللل الموقدين النار» مُخفية «يا طالعين الجبل يا موقدين النار». النظام التقني الثاني يأتي من خلال المعنى الشعري: بمجرد الكشف عن الكلمات الفعلية المخفية وراء الأصوات، يجب أن تخضع لجولة ثانية من التفسير لاستخراج المعنى. على عكس مجتمعات طبقية أخرى، لم تكن القراءة والكتابة والشعر أشياء مخصصة فقط لأولئك الذين يستفيدون من استغلال العمال. كانت الطلاقة في الشعر والتعقيد اللغوي - ولا تزال - *مشاعًا* مشتركًا بين الغالبية العظمى من المجتمع. ومن دون تطعيمها بالزغاريد، تقول الكلمات:

يا طالعين عين الجبل
يا موال الموقدين النار
بين ل يامان يامان عين الهنا يا روح
ما بدي منكي الكم خلعة
ولا بدي ملبوس
بين يامان يامان
عين الهنا يا روح
ما بدي منكي الكم خلعة ولا بدي زنار
بين يامان يامان
عين الهنا يا روح
إلا غزال الذي جوين الكم محبوس
بين يامان يامان
عين الهنا يا روح
إلا غزال الذي جوّين الكم ما يدوم
بين يامان يامان
عين الهنا يا روح

كانت هذه الأغنية تُغنَّى في وداع من يشرعون في رحلات بعيدًا عن الوطن، وكانت في الواقع موجَّهة إلى أولئك الذين أُجبِروا على عدم الذهاب إلى أي مكان: المقاتلين الأسرى لدى حكومة الانتداب وحلفائها الصهاينة. تشير «يا طالعين الجبل» إلى المقاتلين الفلسطينيين الموجودين على الأرض، الذين يستعدون للقدوم في مهمة إنقاذ المقاتلين المسجونين. غنَّتها النساء لإعلام المقاتلين المسجونين، «إلا غزال جوين محبوس»، بالتنبُّه والاستعداد للإفراج عنهم، لأن شَرَكَهم لن يدوم بعد الآن. والإشارة إلى هذه المهمة، التي تعلن بدايتها وتعلن تنفيذها، هي إيقاد النار. فقبل وصول المقاتلين مباشرة، اعتادت النساء على حثِّ «الغزلان» الموجودين في الداخل على التنبُّه إلى النار المشتعلة التي يمكن رؤيتها من خلال شقوق الجدران ونوافذ السجن للاستعداد للهروب.

هناك العديد من الأنواع الأخرى من الأغاني المشفَّرة، ولكل منها نظام التشفير والرسائل الخاص بها. والأغاني المشفَّرة التي لم تعد مستخدمة سياسيًا أصبحت مألوفة ومسجلة بما يكفي للإشارة إليها هنا، في حين أن البعض الآخر في تطور مستمر من خلال ممارسة متواصلة حتى يومنا هذا، وغير مسجلة، وعلى هذا النحو ستبقى. تطورت هذه المشفَّرات كشكل موسيقي خلال محنة الحداثة في فلسطين، في الانتقال من حكم الإمبراطورية العثمانية إلى الاستعمار البريطاني والاستيطان الصهيوني. وكانت استراتيجية جمالية نضالية ولدت من ضرورة مقاومة الحكم الاستعماري والتكنولوجيات التي طوَّرها واختبرها على العالم المستعمَر، على الرغم من عدم توفر التكنولوجيات العسكرية أو الجيوش القوية. لقد نشأت على وجه التحديد من هذا النقص، وهذا الافتقار، وهذه الهشاشة، كشكل جمالي متشابك مع مشروع سياسي. مثل حجر يُرمى باتجاه الجدران المحاصِرة لسجون الانتداب، تجاوزت المشفَّرات المنقوشة في الصوت بُنى المراقبة والحكم والإدارة الاستعمارية. نُظِرَ إلى النساء الفلسطينيات على أنهن قد استُبعِدن من الحياة السياسية واحتُجِزن في المجتمع الأبوي وبالتالي على أنهن لا يشكلن أي تهديد. ونُظِر إليهن أيضًا عرقيا على أنهن نساء أصليات يحملن تقاليد ثقافية مضادة للمنطق الاستعماري، وبالتالي لا يُشكِّلن أي خطر واضح على الحكم الاستعماري. ومع تسلُّل زغاريدهن إلى السجون شديدة الحراسة، لم يُثِر ذلك أي قلق. غناء المشفَّرات وإطلاقها من خلال الأجساد المؤنثة جعلها غير مرئية. اعتُبرت الأصوات دخيلة لأن الأجساد التي أنتجتها كانت تُصوَّر على أنها هامشية اجتماعيًا ضمن العقائد الأبوية الاستعمارية العرقية. هذه الهامشية التي اتَّسمَت بها الأجساد الفلسطينية الأنثوية والمؤنثة، والسلبية المنسوبة إليها، جعلت الصوتَ الذي أنتجته يبدو شبحيًا. لقد نطقن وأدَّين مباشرةً على حدود المؤسسات السجنيَّة الاستعمارية، وتجاوزن الحدود من دون أن يُرى ذلك.

الجـدلية بين الصـوتي والبصـري، الصـور النـاطقة والأصـوات غيـر المـرئية، والتي تـملأ التقاليـد الثـورية الفلسـطينية، نشأت بـالتزامن مـع تبلـور النضـال الـوطني المنـاهض للاستعمـار، ومن داخـل بنية الـكارثة الاستعمـارية الاستيطـانية. وهي تدفـع شـكلًا من أشـكال المعـرفة الغيـر مسجّـل في أنظـمة مُـرتَّبة للتسجيـل والتـوثيق والأرشفة، ولكنهـا مخزَّنة في عضلات المكبـوتين. وبشـكل غـريزي، تنشأ هذه الفئـات من المعـرفة وتعـود للظهـور جيلًا بعـد جيـل كتقاليـد جمـالية للثـورة منقـوشة في الأوعية الثـورية التي نُجسِّـدها، وتنتقـل من خلال التجـربة الاجتمـاعية الحـسية.

تُظهِـر لنـا الاضطرابـات الاجتمـاعية في شـوارع فلسـطين كيف أنـه نـادرًا مـا يُخطَّـط لـلغة الجمـالية، وكيف أنهـا نـادرًا مـا تنطـلق من خلال عمليـات المنـاقشة والقـرار الجمـاعي، ومـع ذلـك فـهي مُنظَمِـرَة في لغة جمـالية منـدمجة في النضـال. إنهـا لغة فقـر. إنهـا لغة هشـاشة. لغة يحملها واقـع منقـوص ومسلـوب باعتبـاره كارثة مستمـرة. لغة تُنشِّـط التخـريب والهـدم وتـحيي موقـع الانتزاع وتعيـد استخـدام وتأهيـل أدوات التشـويه الاستعمـاري الاستيطـاني والجسـد الجريـح المشـوه وصـورِه وتمثيلاتـه. الـلغة باعتبارهـا فائضًـا وحطامًـا. سـواء كانت ابتسـامة أو غـمزة لعـدسة الكاميـرا، أو أغنية مشقَّـرة تتسـلل إلـى زنزانة، أو قصيـدة شـعرية مكتـوبة علـى منديـل ورقي تُهـرَّب خلال سـاعات الزيـارة[٤٤]، أو حفـر حفـرة خـارج الـسجن بملـعقة للإعلان عن الهـروب الكبيـر[٤٥]، أو عزف الموسيقـى في الحانـات والمواخيـر للتغـطية علـى الخطـاب السيـاسي الخاضـع للمـراقبة، أو التحـليق عاليًـا في الهـواء للتغلب علـى الجـدران المحاصِـرة التي تمنـع أجيـالًا من الوصـول إلـى السـماء، كل هذا يتراكـم في هذا السـلبي الذي يستمـر مـرارًا وتكـرارًا. تقليـد المضطهـدين، وجماليـات المكبـوتين.

٤٤
انظر/ي
Layan Kayed, "Prison As a Text," (*Journal for Palestine Studies*) Prisoners' Words.. Springs of Speech, no. 128 (August 2021): 201-6; 1;. Kaleem Hawa, "Like a Bag Trying to Empty," *Parapraxis*, parapraxismagazine.com/articles/like-a-bag-trying-to-empty.

٤٥
الإشارة هنا إلى هروب سجناء من سجن جلبوع في السادس من أيلول/سبتمبر ٢٠٢١، حيث حفر كل من أيهم نايف كممجي، ومحمود عبد الله العارضة، ومحمد قاسم العارضة، ومناضل يعقوب نفيعات، ويعقوب محمود قادري، وزكريا الزبيدي نفقًا للهروب (نفق الحريّة) من أحد أكثر السجون الصهيونية حراسة ومراقبة بالتكنولوجيا المتقدمة، باستخدام ملعقة فقط.

١

ظهرت صورة/وجه/كلمة/زهرة
على شاشتي مرة اخرى، ومن
ثم اختفت عند نقري لها.

٢

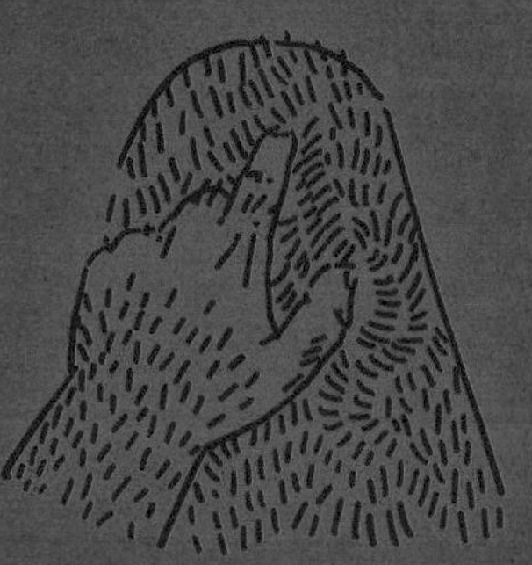

تكرارا، رسمت باصبعي
ملامح تلك الصورة/
وجه/كلمة/زهرة
على فخذي.

٣

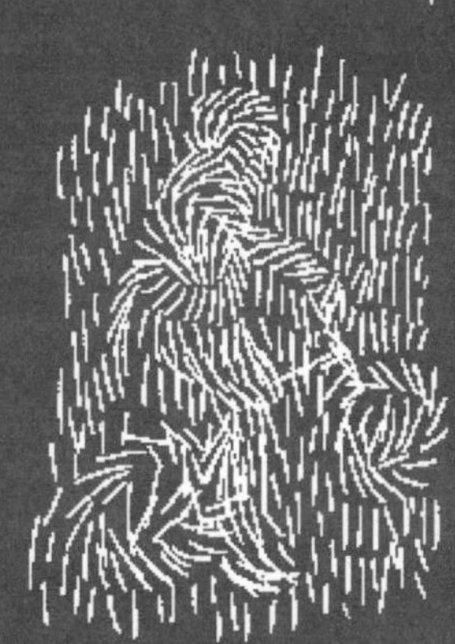

تحولت رسوماتي الى ملامحٍ
باهتةٍ أثر الزيوت على
اطراف اصابعي عند تلامسهن
مع شعيرات فخذي.

٤

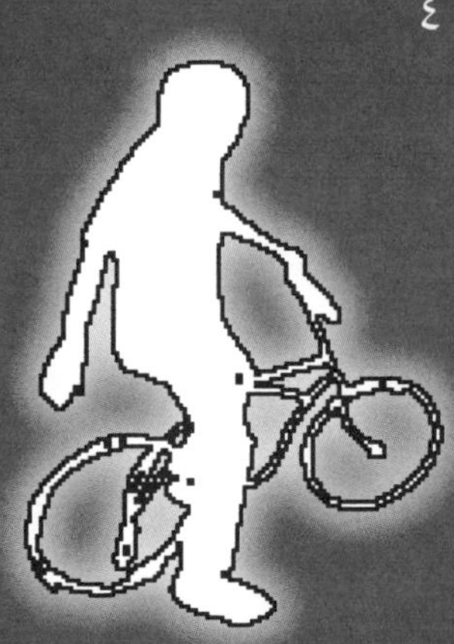

تلك الملامح الباهتة
تحولت الى خطوط
خفيفة مرسومة
على ورقة.

٥

ظهرت هذه الخطوط
المرسومة مرة اخرى
على جسدي كمنقوشات
أزليّة، واستقبلتها
مجموعة من الصور/
وجوه/كلمات/زهور
التي كانت تطاردني
في الماضي.

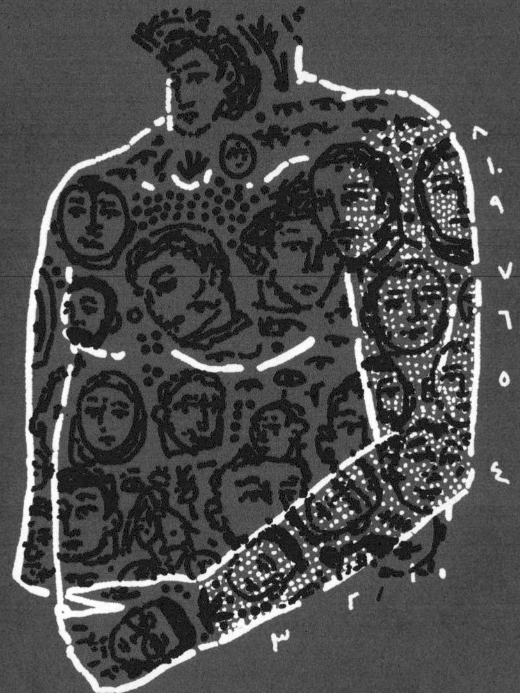

٦

طالما اتساءل حول
ممارسة "تمديد
حياة" تلك الصور/
وجوه/كلمات/زهور

مهلة اطول لتبقى في
مخيلتي،

حتى يطول بقاءها
قبل ان تختفي؟

٧

استعملت هاتفي لاصور
الصورة/وجه/كلمة/
زهرة

عادت هذه الصورة
الى شاشتي.

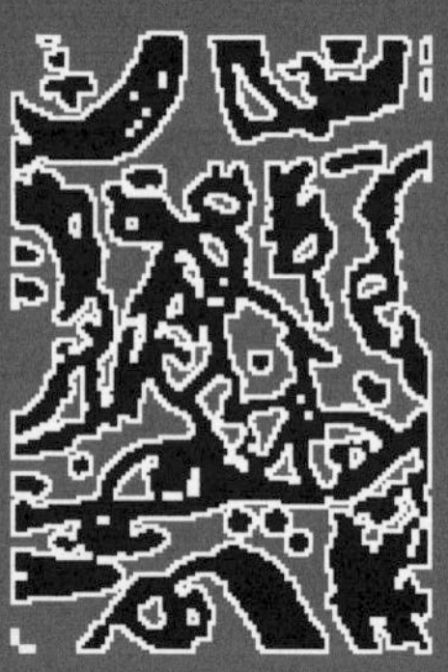

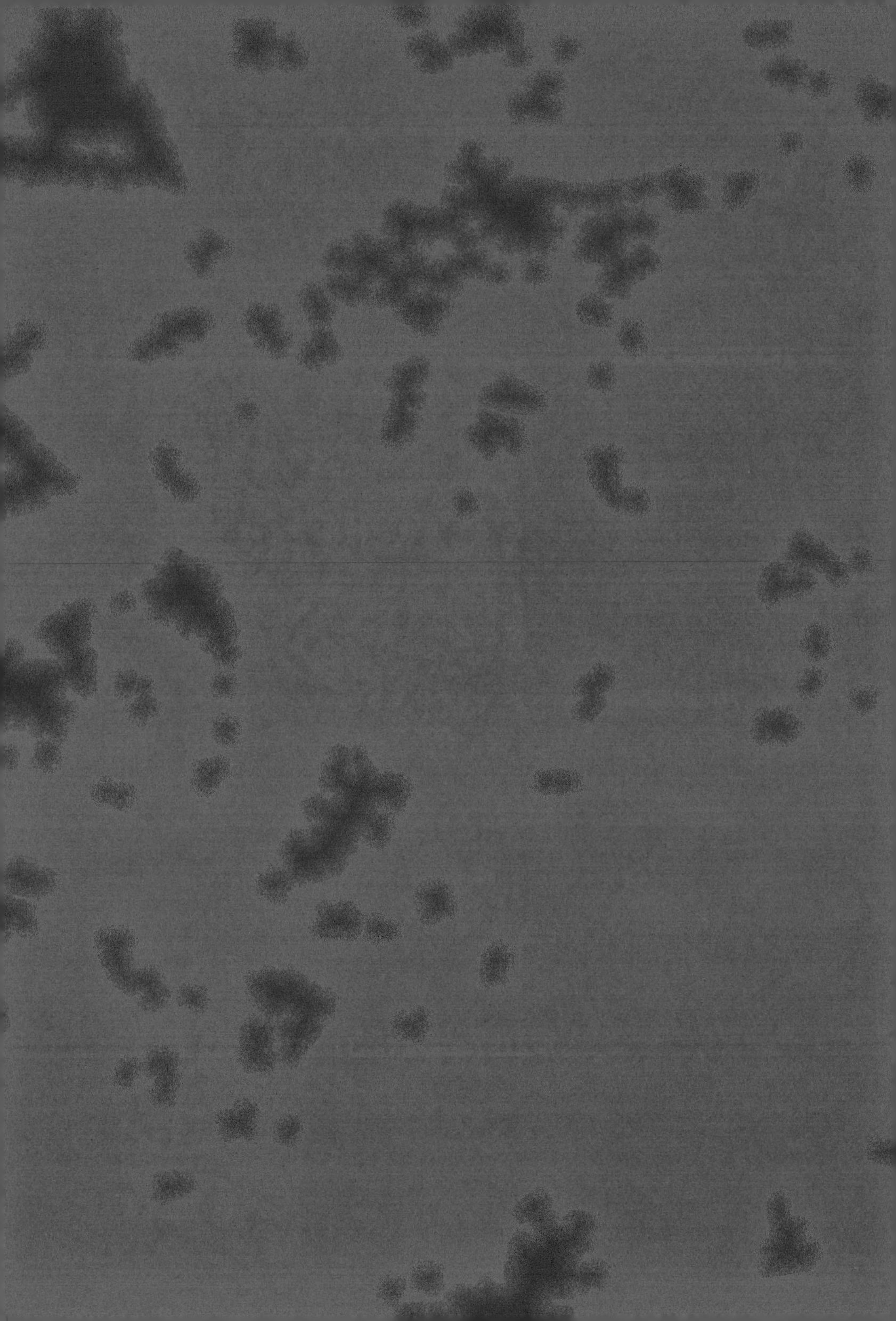